CONTENTS

BITTERSWEET HARVESTS FOR GLOBAL SUPERMARKETS:

Challenges in

Latin America's

Agricultural

WORLD
RESOURCES
INSTITUTE

Export Boom

August 1995

Lori Ann Thrupp

with Gilles Bergeron
and William F. Waters

Institute of Latin American Studies
31 Tavistock Square
London WC1H 9HA

1 3 0 6 0

16. SEP. 1999

Library of Congress Cataloging-in-Publication Data

Thrupp, Lori Ann.
  Bittersweet harvests for global supermarkets : sustainability and equity in Latin America's agroexport boom / by Lori Ann Thrupp, with
Gilles Bergeron and William Waters.
    p. cm.
  Includes bibliographical references.
  ISBN 1-56973-029-6 (alk. paper)
  1. Produce trade—Latin America. 2. Floriculture—Latin America.
3. Exports—Latin America. 4. Agriculture and state—Latin America.
5. Sustainable agriculture—Latin America. 6. Agriculture—Economic
aspects—Latin America. I. Bergeron, Gilles. II. Waters, William F.
III. Title.
HD9014.L32T48 1995
382′.41′098—dc20   95-14320
                                                                  CIP

Kathleen Courrier
Publications Director

Brooks Belford
Marketing Manager

Hyacinth Billings
Production Manager

Lomangino Studio; photo by Sam Fields
Cover Design

Each World Resources Institute Report represents a timely, scholarly treatment
of a subject of public concern. WRI takes responsibility for choosing the study
topics and guaranteeing its authors and researchers freedom of inquiry. It also
solicits and responds to the guidance of advisory panels and expert reviewers.
Unless otherwise stated, however, all the interpretation and findings set forth in
WRI publications are those of the authors.

v

FOREWORD

Some Latin American countries have shipped their summertime fruits North for thirty years or more, but, until recently, these exotic exports were a trickle aimed mainly at the wealthy. Decades ago, a winter-weary Boston housewife might now and then have dented the weekly grocery budget by visiting a fancy food shop for Chilean raspberries or Ecuadorean mangos, just to offer her family delectable evidence that February cannot last forever. Over the last ten years, though, the trickle has become a flood that reaches most U.S. supermarkets, not just the trendy urban shops.

Today's well-stocked markets are the result of an agroexport boom promoted by multinational agencies to increase earnings in Central and South America. Exports of these new and diverse crops have grown explosively. Is this strategy a success? What are the social and environmental consequences? Lori Ann Thrupp, a senior associate in WRI's Center for International Development and Environment, assisted by Gilles Bergeron (a research fellow at the International Food Policy Research Institute), and William Waters (a sociology professor at the Universidad San Francisco de Quito) takes on these important questions in *Bittersweet Harvests for Global Supermarkets: Challenges in Latin America's Agricultural Export Boom.*

Dr. Thrupp and her colleagues trace the history of efforts to promote the growth of so-called "non-traditional agricultural exports" during the early 1980s. As part of structural adjustment and trade liberalization strategies, these new crops were to spur economic growth, build businesses, and create jobs in poor rural areas throughout Latin America. In some ways, the authors note, these efforts have succeeded. In Ecuador, for instance, exports of exotic

vii

fruits, vegetables, and flowers grew fifteenfold in volume and thirty-fold in value between 1985 and 1991. Jobs are booming too: Colombia's flower plantations employ about 80,000 people, 80 percent of them women. But the market success has come at a cost in workers' health, inequitable distribution of benefits, and environmental degradation in many of the exporting countries.

In assessing environmental costs, *Bittersweet Harvests* stresses excessive pesticide use as a major concern, for economic as well as social reasons. Even at today's levels, pesticide use is damaging the health of farmworkers, especially those who work on flower plantations. In Colombia and Ecuador, for instance, women who work in greenhouses suffer high miscarriage rates, recurrent headaches, and dizzy spells caused by exposure to toxic chemicals. Workers' health will decline even more if pesticide use escalates, an ever-present threat since the pests that survive eventually breed resistance into succeeding generations, tempting landowners to either raise the dosage or turn to even more potent chemicals. The economic cost can be steep for investors and landowners when pesticide residues are so high that crops are turned back at the U.S. border: in the past ten years, this has cost them more than $95 million.

While non-traditional agroexports have been commercially successful and have made some people rich, the authors find that the export boom has not produced the anticipated improvements in income and living standards for the many who are poor. Although these new crops can be grown on much smaller plots of land than such traditional exports as coffee and bananas, peasant farmers are often shut out of these markets because they lack access to credit, technology, and information. Indeed, most of the profits from these crops are reaped by affluent investors or multinational firms. Moreover, many of the jobs created by this non-traditional form of agriculture are insecure and sporadic, with no work in some parts of the year and double shifts in others. The women workers who make up the bulk of this new work force are often paid lower wages than men for the same work and often lack legally-mandated job rights.

On balance, say the authors, this export boom seems to be doing little to mitigate the poverty that plagues rural households throughout the region. These "new" crops offer new hopes, but too often they are being developed along patterns like those found in traditional coffee, sugarcane, and banana plantations. Fortunately, Dr. Thrupp and her colleagues discovered, innovative initiatives to prevent or mitigate social and environmental problems and to make these crops more economically sustainable are afoot in many places. It remains to be seen whether NGO and government efforts to improve farmworkers' training, benefits, and opportunities and to support small-farmer organic produce cooperatives will turn the tide, but they are steps toward spreading the benefits of export crops and greening production.

If sustainable development means anything, Dr. Thrupp and her colleagues maintain, it means not just conserving the natural resource base, but also ensuring a better life for the rural poor. Based on research findings and on workshop discussions with small farmers, farmworkers, and government policy-makers about the issues and policy implications that this booming export market raises, the authors developed six recommendations that would help make non-traditional agroexport-oriented strategies more equitable and sustainable:

1. Promote participatory approaches, focussing on the inclusion of poor farmers and workers in agricultural development decision-making and in socioeconomic opportunities.

2. Build a policy environment to mitigate or avoid adverse impacts of these agroexports and to support and multiply sustainable and equitable patterns of agricultural development.

3. Promote and develop sustainable agricultural technologies and practices, stressing integrated pest management, organic practices, and diversity, through changes by all actors in the production-market chain.

4. Build a better balance in policy attention to local vs. export production, placing priority on alleviating hunger and fulfilling local food security needs.

5. Increase the empowerment and status of poor producers and workers in production and marketing to overcome biases in market conditions and to promote equitable alternatives.

6. Increase information on the market conditions and impacts of agroexports, and improve access to such information for a wide audience of interested people.

Bittersweet Harvests complements the analyses and recommendations set forth in such previous WRI studies as *Agricultural Policy and Sustainability: Case Studies from India, Chile, the Philippines, and the United States* and *Pesticides, Rice Productivity, and Farmers' Health: An Economic Assessment.* To follow up on one of *Bittersweet Harvests'* main recommendations, Dr. Thrupp is now analyzing how integrated pest management and related practices are working around the world to reduce pesticide use while ensuring profitable harvests.

We would like to thank the U.S. Agency for International Development for helping underwrite the research reflected in *Bittersweet Harvests.* The agency's financial support has helped the authors show governments and assistance agencies how to design and implement agricultural policies that will benefit exporting countries—and their farmworkers and landowners—economically and environmentally over the long haul.

Jonathan Lash
President
World Resources Institute

ACKNOWLEDGMENTS

This report is the outcome of a collaborative effort involving many people and institutions. I am particularly thankful for the cooperation and contribution of the Institute of Nutrition of Central America and Panama, Centro Mesoamericano de Estudios sobre Tecnologías Apropriadas, the Instituto de Ciencia y Tecnología Agrícola in Guatemala, the Universidad San Francisco de Quito, and Centro de Planificación y Estudios Sociales in Ecuador.

I would like to thank WRI colleagues Thomas Fox, Walter Arensberg, Walter Reid, Paul Faeth, Robert Repetto, Robert Blake, Kristin Schafer, Aaron Zazueta, Bruce Cabarle, Keith Kozloff, and Elizabeth Cook for their careful reviews and thoughtful comments throughout the writing process. I am very grateful to Gilles Bergeron and William Waters for their contribution to the project, to research assistants Karin Perkins and Julie Merrill, to Robert McCoy and Kathleen Courrier for their skillful editing, to Hyacinth Billings and Samantha Fields for publication production, to Olinda Ramos and Maura Paternoster for administrative assistance, and to Daniel Nielsen and Steven Lanou for assistance on graphics. Special thanks are also due to Robert Bailey, Bradford Barham, Roberto Caceras, Michael Carter, Michael Conroy, Richard Fisher, James Fox, Raul Harari, Kevin Healy, Polly Hoppin, Maarten Immink, David Kaimowitz, Elizabeth Katz, Douglas Murray, Paula Palmer, Victor Puac, Jorge Rodriguez, Peter Rosset, Lucia Salamea, Kenneth Swanberg, Kenneth Weiss, and Wayne Williams whose valuable reviews, suggestions, and information were appreciated. Other groups deserving acknowledgment for their input include AVANCSO, ASINDES, COINDE, and PROEXAG in Guatemala, and PROEXANT, FUNDAGRO, and COMUNIDEC in Ecuador.

The U.S. Agency for International Development (USAID) helped support this project. I am thankful to individuals working in USAID, particularly Bruce Brower, Angel Chiri, Howard Clark, James Hester, Peter Lapera, Aida Lefebre, Fausto Maldonado, William Sugrue, Roberta Von Haeften, Kenneth Wiegand, John Wilson, Clarence Zuvekas, and who provided information, support, or useful ideas. Last but not least, I greatly appreciate the participation of many women and men who are directly involved in agricultural production and natural resource management in Latin America; they made possible the research and the workshops that formed the basis of this project.

L.A.T.

OVERVIEW

Responding to critical economic and social challenges—deepening debt and recession, widespread hunger and unemployment, growing gaps between rich and poor, and ecological degradation—the countries of Latin America and the Caribbean have struggled over the past decade to vitalize their economies and to forge new patterns of development. Attempts to bring about changes are diverse and sometimes divergent; they range from regional market liberalization policies to local-level environmental initiatives. In agriculture, the production of diverse high-value crops for export has been strongly fostered by development agencies in attempts to stimulate economic growth. But concerns are emerging about whether and how this export-oriented strategy benefits poor hungry people, increases food security, or is ecologically appropriate. More generally, does it contribute to "sustainable development"— furthering environmental soundness, social equity, and economic growth assured over time? If so, how? And if not, why?

Export agriculture is by no means new to Latin America and the Caribbean. Historically, the traditional export sector has dominated the dualistic agrarian structure that characterizes the region, coexisting with numerous small-scale farmers who produce food for local markets and for their own families.[1] Most agricultural land is in large plantations dedicated to traditional export commodities—including sugarcane, coffee, bananas, and cotton—that have generated substantial export earnings and profitable businesses for many decades. But these lucrative activities have also contributed to social inequities and environmental degradation, and they have proven to be economically unsustainable as their prices and terms of trade periodically plummeted.[2] Some studies suggest that focusing investments in such cash crops has hindered local food security.[3] These traditional export-production systems both contributed to and suffered from the serious socioeconomic crisis of the 1980's in the region.

Against this gloomy backdrop, new export-expansion efforts have been undertaken in recent years, focusing on diverse new crops. Business in fashionable high-value agricultural export products is booming in Latin America and the Caribbean, and it is growing in Africa and Asia as well. These products—fresh and processed fruits and juices, vegetables, flowers, and nuts—are commonly known as *non-traditional agricultural exports* (NTAEs), as distinct from traditional exports of coffee, bananas, cotton, and sugarcane. *(See Box 1.)* Over the past decade, such exports have

---

Box 1. Clarification of Terms

The term *non-traditional agroexports* describes a group of diverse agricultural export products, excluding such "traditional" export products as coffee, bananas, cotton, beef, and sugarcane. An export is considered non-traditional if it: (1) was not traditionally produced in a particular country; (2) was traditionally produced for domestic consumption but now is exported; or (3) is a traditional product now exported to a new market. In general, these crops share characteristics of high per unit value and high intensity in production.

The use of the concept "non-traditional" is relative. Some products that are "traditional" exports in one country are "non-traditional" in another. For example, grapes are now traditional in Chile, but not in other Latin American countries. Given this complexity, some analysts prefer to use the term "high value" exports when referring to these emerging diversified crops.

Source: Bradford Barham, M. Clark, E. Katz, and R. Schurman, "Nontraditional Agricultural Exports in Latin America," *Latin American Research Review*, 1992, vol. 11, no. 26.

---

fared much better in international trade than other products. While the value and growth of export earnings in coffee, cocoa, and cotton plummeted during the 1980s, developing countries' exports in the diverse high-value non-traditional products grew, on average by 4 to 11 percent annually.[4] World trade in "edible horticultural products" (fruits and vegetables) alone ($40.3 billion) exceeded that for cereals ($38.6 billion) in 1988–89.[5] Thanks to this growth of global food markets, consumers in industrial countries can now enjoy a broad variety of fresh products year round.

Many Latin American and Caribbean countries have experienced rapid growth rates in these non-traditional export crops, as shown in Figures 1 and 2. In Central America, the value of NTAEs increased on average by 17.2 percent annually between 1985 and 1992; and in South America (excluding Brazil), the annual growth figure during this time was 48 percent.[6] The rates of NTAE growth from 1984 through 1989 in Chile, Costa Rica, and Guatemala were 222 percent, 348 percent, and 78 percent, respectively.[7] Fresh fruits, vegetables, and flowers rank among the fastest-growing NTAEs. In Ecuador, for example, the flower business increased an impressive 15-fold in volume and 30-fold in value between 1985 and 1991.[8] Although currently these crops account for a small percentage of total export values (e.g. 12 percent in South America), and a small fraction of total land area in most of Latin America, the rates of growth and unit values are nonetheless remarkable.

The main factors inducing this rapid growth are changes in international trade policies and technologies, shifts in dietary preferences and increased consumer incomes in industrial countries, and greater penetration of transnational food companies in the South. The expansion of NTAEs has been supported by international financial and development agencies, particularly the U.S. Agency for International Development (USAID) and the World Bank, and by national government institutions, in attempts to increase economic growth, repay debts, and reduce reliance on exports of such traditional crops as bananas, coffee, sugar cane, and beef. For these agencies, promoting cash crop exports is a central part of trade liberalization and structural adjustment policies.

Indeed, the growth of non-traditional agribusiness has been highly profitable for some enterprises in the South, foreign in-

3

Figure 1. Map of Latin America and the Caribbean Showing Countries with Rapid NTAE Growth

Countries that have experienced rapid growth of nontraditional agroexport products (NTAEs) in the 1980s and 1990s

Source: Inter-American Development Bank (IDB), *Economic and Social Progress in Latin America* (IDB, Washington, D.C., 1993).

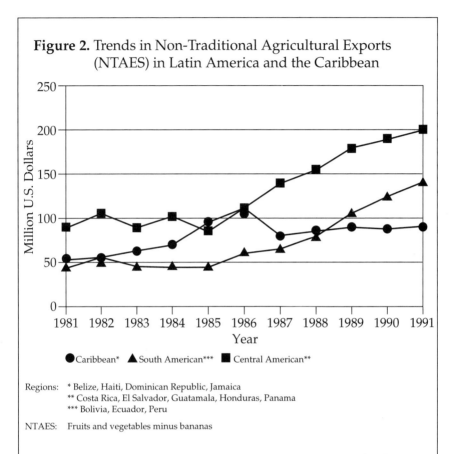

Figure 2. Trends in Non-Traditional Agricultural Exports (NTAES) in Latin America and the Caribbean

●Caribbean* ▲South American*** ■Central American**

Regions: * Belize, Haiti, Dominican Republic, Jamaica
           ** Costa Rica, El Salvador, Guatamala, Honduras, Panama
           *** Bolivia, Ecuador, Peru

NTAES: Fruits and vegetables minus bananas

Source: Robert Van Haeften, William Goodwin, and Clarence Zuvekas, "LAC Development Trends: Background for New Strategy," based on Agrostat data of the Food and Agriculture Organization, (Washington, D.C.: U.S. Agency for International Development, 1993).

vestors, and transnational food corporations. Most of the products are more valuable than traditional exports and local crops. In recent years, the international price per metric ton of fresh fruit and vegetables has averaged $500 while the prices for grains have ranged from $75 to $175 per metric ton.[9] The business is very profitable for those who succeed. Many of the NTAE crops are labor intensive and have generated a significant number of jobs, particularly for women. By diversifying exports, national economies reduce reliance on traditional sectors, spread risks, and broaden technical capacity. Furthermore, Northern consumers are enjoying these new products at prices that are dropping over time.

These economic indicators have led some observers to judge this NTAE boom a success. However, while the growth of NTAEs has some undeniable advantages and elements of commercial success, it also has "bitter" dimensions. Evidence from several countries reveals that the production and marketing of NTAEs entail considerable environmental and social costs, inequities, and risks, generally greater than those in the production of foods for traditional local markets. These adverse outcomes reflect similar patterns of previous export booms.

For example, the very high inputs of pesticides commonly used in most NTAEs have impaired workers' health, posed risks to consumers from residues in food, brought on pest resistance and environmental disruptions, and consequently, elevated costs. One of the most visible and alarming manifestations of pesticide overuse is the accumulation of residues in the products. When importing countries' residue tolerance standards are violated, producers and exporters must pay penalties and suffer losses. NTAE fruits and vegetables imported into the United States between 1984 and 1994 from ten Latin American and Caribbean countries have been subject to approximately *14,000 detentions* of tested produce by the Food and Drug Administration because they exceeded pesticide residue standards. As a result, estimated total losses to the producer countries have totalled *over $95 million,* as shown in Table 1.[10] Workers' exposure to highly toxic chemicals also presents serious problems on NTAE farms, especially for women engaged in flower production. Adverse labor conditions, such as unfair wages and lack of contractual agreements with employers, are also common in this sector.[11]

Furthermore, the fruits of NTAE production are often inequitably distributed. Wealthy investors and foreign distributors reap most of the immediate benefits, while poor farmers usually have difficulties entering and competing effectively in this market. Although in some countries such as Guatemala poorer farmers

Table 1. Summary of U.S. FDA Detentions for Pesticide
Residues in Shipments of Fruits and Vegetables
Imported from Selected Latin America, FY 1984–94

	Total number of detentions[a]	Total estimated $US value of shipments detained[b]
Chile	666	$9,475,000
Colombia	79	200,000
Costa Rica	102	411,000
Dominican Republic	2,259	11,257,000
Ecuador	35	158,000
El Salvador	39	977,000
Guatemala	3,168	17,972,000
Honduras	66	269,000
Jamaica	150	583,000
Mexico	7,429	54,589,000

Source: WRI analysis of U.S. Food and Drug Administration data.

a. Shipments are detained for pesticide testing when a random sampling of a small portion of a shipment indicates potential violations of FDA regulations, or when a product from a certain country is under automatic detention, as is currently the case with snow peas from Guatemala and a handful of products from the Dominican Republic. Many detained shipments are released for entry into the U.S. following testing.

b. Values are not exact due to possible minor inconsistencies or errors in measurement and calculation.

benefitted from NTAE production, particularly during the 1980s, evidence suggests that the returns from NTAEs seldom reach disadvantaged peoples to help alleviate hunger. In some cases, the increasing emphasis on export crops can detract from local food security. Some analysts note the irony of increasing investments in producing specialty foods and flowers for foreigners—mostly middle-to-upper class consumers—while hunger and environmental degradation persist in the region of cultivation.

Economic uncertainties also cloud the outlook for many NTAEs. Prices are highly volatile, inputs are expensive, market requirements extremely demanding and sometimes prohibitive, competition is intense, and export windows are very narrow. Providing these goods to Northern consumers in a timely way requires complicated production technologies and marketing systems. The necessity for high levels of capital presents major challenges for many producers, especially for poor small-scale farmers. For these reasons, high growth and profitability cannot always be sustained in many NTAE crops.

These drawbacks, many of which also plague the traditional export sector, call into question the sustainability and equity of this agroexport development strategy. Indeed, NTAE growth has not always resulted in the anticipated improvements in income and living standards for the poor. This assessment does *not* suggest that these export-oriented growth strategies are inherently unsustainable and inequitable. But many of the patterns and policies within this overall strategy raise concerns requiring attention.

Some NTAE producers and institutions have responded to these dilemmas. New initiatives have included the development of organic export crops such as organic coffee, quinoa, or cocoa, that entail less pesticides—thereby opening up new "green" markets. Several attempts have been made to develop integrated pest management and pesticide monitoring for NTAEs, and a few efforts have been undertaken to address social considerations—for instance, by supporting small farmers associations or improving labor conditions. Such efforts have promising potential, but so far have been very limited in size and impact.

In *Bittersweet Harvests for Global Supermarkets*, key characteristics and challenges in the recent diversification of agricultural exports in developing countries are explained, the salient socioeconomic and environmental impacts of NTAEs in Latin America are assessed, and the policies and actions needed to address dilemmas and strengthen opportunities are identified. The report focuses mainly on NTAEs in Latin America—especially high-value fruits, vegetables, and flowers—highlighting evidence from field studies in Ecuador and Guatemala. Rather than to simply compare nontraditional and traditional crops, the goal here is to assess NTAEs in relation to broader development needs and policy challenges. The findings grow out of collaborative research and original field surveys conducted with institutions in Latin America (on pesticide use, pest control, and labor conditions for women workers), policy and economic analysis, and participatory workshops. (*See Appendix 2* on methodology.)

The analysis is presented through a lens of an overall strategic objective of *broad-based sustainable development*. In agriculture, this means ensuring equitable opportunities for poor farmers and rural workers and guaranteeing food security, as well as developing agricultural practices that are economically viable and environmentally sound, as depicted in Figure 3. This development framework is needed in order to overcome the critical socioeconomic and ecological crises of the late 20th century. Moreover, it has also been endorsed, at least in principle, by many public and private institutions and donors that work in development, including those that promote NTAEs.[12]

This study reflects an appreciation of the political-economic context, particularly by revealing how the historically rooted economic policies and social structures undergird the growth and impacts of agroexports. It also sheds light on the important current debate about the impacts of trade expansion on the environment. Analysis along these lines shows that the outcomes of NTAE ventures partly reflect policies and investments aimed at gaining short-term economic profits and facilitating structural adjustment and market liberalization. Seldom do these policies integrate sustainability and social equity concerns.

The conclusions of the report suggest that changes in agroexport growth policies and practices are needed at all levels to prevent problems and increase benefits in this sector. Development

9

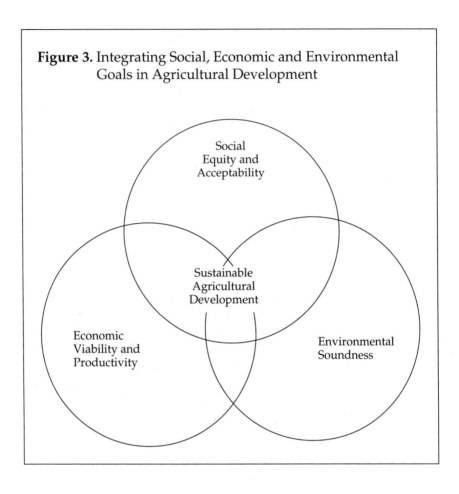

Figure 3. Integrating Social, Economic and Environmental Goals in Agricultural Development

agencies, government and non-government institutions, researchers, private enterprise, consumers, and laborers all need to be involved in making changes, to work toward sustainable and equitable agricultural development.

One of the key policy recommendations—for institutions, policy-makers, and producers in both North America and Latin America—is the full integration of environmental incentives and regulations and of the social needs of the poor into agricultural/economic growth policies. *(See Figure 3.)* Accordingly, programs must be redesigned to help expand equitable opportunities for the poor and to eliminate policies, such as incentives for pesticide use, that can lead to environmental degradation. Broadening the base of agricultural development also requires better balancing export strategies and local food-production policies by increasing political will and investments in improving local food security to alleviate hunger.

Producers, non-government organizations (NGOs), and agro-chemical suppliers, as well as government agencies and development organizations—need to make additional reforms, including the development of sustainable production methods (integrated pest management and organic practices, for instance), and the promotion of diverse indigenous crops that have high market potential. These groups must work to strengthen local farmer organizations and technical services to build economic opportunities and bargaining power for the rural poor. The findings also show the importance of enhancing diversity of production and crop varieties at all levels, the participation of small producers and workers in decision-making concerning agricultural development strategies, the protection of workers' rights and health, and enforcement of labor laws. Increasing information on NTAE market conditions and impacts, and improving access to such information are also urgent needs requiring research and monitoring capacities.

In an increasingly interdependent world market system, it is essential for Northern consumers to adjust those of their consumption patterns that affect export production—for instance, by buying produce that is not "blemish-free." Consumers' acceptance of less-than-perfect looking produce gives them better or equal nutritional quality, while reducing pressure on producers to use pesticides. Regulatory agencies, marketing businesses, and import companies must also work together to relax aesthetic standards and develop consistent regulations in ways that can induce sustainable and safe production practices.

More fundamentally, underlying causes of problems—tied to inequitable agrarian structures in Latin America and financial pressures from international development agencies—need to be addressed. The dominant economic policies and practices oriented toward short-term, unfettered agroexport growth need to be balanced with policies and long-term goals for environmentally-sound production, socially-sensitive development, and empowerment of the poor. These kinds of changes are needed not only for social or ethical reasons. They can also contribute to broad national economic goals and political stability in the region.

I.
THE POLITICAL-ECONOMIC CONTEXT OF AGRICULTURAL DEVELOPMENT

Agriculture has formed a foundation for Latin American and Caribbean economies for many centuries. Over time, agricultural development in the region has depended on a rich diversity of natural resources, as well as changes in farming systems, productivity improvements, and the labor of millions of people. The historically rooted agrarian structure is characterized by dualism and a highly inequitable distribution of resources in most of the region's countries: a large-scale capitalized agricultural sector (*latifundia*) that has concentrated control of most of the agricultural land and resources coexists with a sector of millions of poor small-scale farmers (*minifundia*) who produce for local markets and their own subsistence.[13] In Central America, for example, less than 1 percent of all farm owners (large estates over 350 hectares) control nearly 40 percent of the total farmland; on the other hand, small farms (under 3 hectares) account for 78 percent of the total farms, but occupy only 11 percent of all agricultural land.[14] In some areas of Latin America, the rural tenure structure has become more heterogeneous and complex over time, encompassing many middle-sized farms as well; but, overall, dualism still prevails.[15] The rich and poor farming sectors are often linked through labor markets, but these relationships are unequal. Numerous people have been excluded from the benefits of economic growth and displaced on to unproductive lands partly as large-scale enterprises expand and asymmetric development processes unfold.[16]

Over the last half century, many Latin American and Caribbean economies have been based on earnings from traditional agricul-

13

tural exports, including coffee, bananas, sugarcane, and cocoa. Large plantations of most of these commodities date back to the late 1800s and early 1900s.[17] Over time, the countries diversified into cotton, beef, and cocoa for export. During the 1960s and 1970s, most countries adopted an inward-oriented development strategy of Import Substitution Industrialization (ISI). Nevertheless, overall economic growth has continued to depend considerably on exports.[18]

The dominance of export agriculture has had significant repercussions on the social structure and economic development paths of the region. In most Latin American countries, the traditional agroexport economy is typified by the prevalence of large-scale, capital-intensive monocultural plantations, high inputs of imported technologies, particularly agrochemicals, dependency on Northern markets, and exploitation of natural resources and of low-wage labor forces. Traditional agroexport enterprises, which occupy large portions of the best agricultural land areas, have a long and influential history in the region. Much of traditional agribusiness in bananas has been controlled by transnational companies, and foreign capital has been important in the production of other exports as well.[19]

Export agribusinesses have enjoyed dynamic growth and high profitability over time, increasing foreign exchange earnings and investment in the region. They have generated jobs, ancillary businesses, and infrastructure development. However, the booms have been short-lived, often followed by economic "busts," as prices of export commodities have fallen periodically. Dependency on a small group of traditional agricultural exports has made Latin American economies vulnerable to unstable market conditions. Exporting nations have suffered from trade protectionism, fluctuating (often declining) terms of trade, and unequal exchange relations.[20]

The growth of traditional agroexports has also reinforced and exacerbated disparities in the distribution of land and other resources.[21] Large landowning enterprises have captured most of the benefits of the export booms, while thousands of small farm households have been unable to benefit or have become low-wage laborers.[22] In many cases, the surplus earnings from these cash crops have not contributed to socially beneficial investment, but have been extracted by foreign companies or transferred to the North through unequal exchange.[23] Some analysts have also shown that the focus on increasing export cash crops can sometimes hinder local food security.[24]

Traditional agroexport systems have also caused serious environmental degradation throughout most of the region.[25] In cotton and banana plantations, for example, overuse of chemical pesticides resulted in serious pesticide resistance problems, impairment of human health, and harmful accumulation of residues in the environment and products, while soils were often exploited to the point of becoming infertile. At the same time, historical records repeatedly document unjust treatment of the labor force along with marginalization of poor small farmers.[26]

The cattle boom in Central America had similar consequences. Although owners of large ranches gained immediate profits during the beef boom, tens of thousands of peasant farmers were displaced as pasture was converted to farmland. This conversion process also led to severe soil erosion, landslides, siltation of water sources, and flooding.[27] Collectively, these adverse ecological and social impacts harm human welfare and undermine production and profits, sometimes resulting in bankruptcy of the agribusinesses.

During the early 1980s, most Latin American and Caribbean countries suffered serious economic and social crises characterized by growing external debts, poverty, unemployment, and widening disparities between the rich and the poor. By the end of the 1980s, the so-called "lost decade," an estimated 108 million people—one quarter of the total population—lived in households that earned less than a dollar a day per person.[28] Hunger and malnutrition are still pervasive; almost six million children are underweight in the region.[29] These dismal trends, partly tied to global recession, have been aggravated by nations' overdependency on a few agroexport commodities.

Although the worst of the recession has passed in this region, agriculture continues to contribute to and to suffer from increasing deterioration of the natural resources. In the 1980s, severe and moderate soil erosion affected more than two million square kilometers in Latin America.[30] Central America has lost an estimated 30 percent of cultivable land because of erosion, and some 70 percent of the productive arid lands of South America and Mexico have been undermined by desertification.[31] In Ecuador, severe soil erosion affects 12 percent of agricultural land,[32] and in Guatemala, 35 percent of the total land is degraded, undermining fertility and productivity.[33] Deforestation of marginal land unsuitable for agriculture has also accelerated in recent decades, compounding resource degradation.[34] Indiscriminate use of pesticides has been widespread, particularly in the agroexport sector.[35] These trends in resource degradation have exacerbated poverty as well.

In sum, these pervasive dilemmas in the region have interlinked economic, social, political, and environmental elements. They spawn a downward spiral of socioeconomic decline and widen the gaps between the rich and the poor. These conditions are deeply-rooted in political-economic asymmetries and in the prevailing development models and policies established by foreign and national institutions.

II.

THE RISE OF NEW AGROEXPORT STRATEGIES: POLICIES, MARKETS, AND INSTITUTIONAL CONDITIONS

A. The Remarkable Boom of Non-traditional Agricultural Products

In response to the serious social and economic dilemmas of the 1980's, new development policies and initiatives have emerged, emerged, ranging from market-based growth models to environmental conservation strategies. The dominant initiatives are tied to structural adjustment and economic stabilization policies, the opening of markets, and growth in exports and the private sector as part of the world trade liberalization backed by the international financial institutions.[36]

The expansion of agricultural exports, especially the diversification into non-traditional, high-value products such as fruits, vegetables, flowers, nuts, and oils, is a central part of these dominant strategies. Agricultural diversification is not a new concept to Latin America. Throughout the 20th century, the countries of the region have broadened their production to some extent, adding cotton, tobacco, and beef to traditional crops of sugar, cocoa, bananas, and coffee. Yet, what were once "new" crops are now considered "traditional." Diversification efforts throughout the region have expanded into a much wider variety of both fresh and processed high-value commodities, which are considered non-traditional.[37] The growth of these agroexports is often equated with agricultural modernization, interpreted by many as increases in productivity and the development of enterpreneurial capability.[38]

Chile, Mexico, and Colombia were pioneers in the booms of high value fruits, vegetables, and flowers. For example, Chile's renowned surge in high-value fruit exports started in the 1960s and continues to be boosted by government support, aggressive business expansion by large companies, and support from U.S. and European governments and investors.[39] Between 1962 and 1988, Chile's fruit exports increased in volume from 36,017 million tons to 972,326 million tons—a 26-fold increase; the value increased from $19.9 million to $473 million (in constant 1985 dollars). Grape exports increased 52-fold in volume and 46-fold in value during these years.[40] Following a similar path, Mexico's early boom in the fresh vegetable sector occurred in the 1960s, controlled largely by American transnational corporations (TNCs) operating south of the Rio Grande River. Next came the growth of large agribusinesses for exporting strawberries and tomatoes in the late 1970's and 1980's.[41] The volume of external sales of Mexico's vegetables increased by 136 percent in 1970 and 1987, growing from 757 thousand to 1.8 million tons; and export value increased by 270 percent in this period.[42]

Colombia's cut-flower export industry also blossomed in the early 1970's, started by a U.S. company called Floramerica that virtually controlled the industry for several years. Between 1967 and 1974, many new companies entered the business and the value of Colombia's flower exports increased over 500 percent, from $113 million to $678 million.[43] By 1980, it became the world's second largest flower exporter (after the Netherlands)—a position it still retains.[44] Today, there are over 350 companies in Colombia's savanna region, which in 1994 produced over 3.5 billion flowers worth over $350 million.[45]

These early developments of high-value exports entailed enormous investments in irrigation and infrastructure, plus high operating costs for machinery and chemicals, fueled largely by the influx of capital from the United States. The remarkable increase was also bolstered by sectoral and macroeconomic policy reforms, including fiscal incentives, exchange rate policies, and price and commercial policies.[46] The growth of these export enterprises has also relied on the exploitation of low-wage labor and natural resources—factors that need to be considered when appraising the impacts. (*See Chapter 4.*)

The models set by these early booms have been followed by other non-traditional agroexport strategies throughout the region. This report refers mainly to such high-value crops as flowers, fresh and processed fruits (particularly mangos, melon, pineapples, passion fruit, berries), and vegetables (broccoli, snow peas, asparagus, mini-squash, artichokes)—all of which have experienced rapid growth *(see Figure 2 and Table 2)*. Other rapidly growing non-traditional exports not covered in this report include shrimp, non-timber forest products, and manufactured goods produced in *maquiladora* (assembly) industries.

B. International Economic Policies and Development Agencies

Underlying the NTAE boom are significant international, regional, and national policies, along with changing conditions in global

---

Table 2. Central America: Value and Structure of Exports, 1979 and 1988 in Million U.S. Dollars and Percentages

	Traditional[a]		Percentages Central America		Non-traditional		Total Dollars		Percentage Change 1979–
	1979	1988	1979	1988	1979	1988	1979	1988	1988
Costa Rica	64.2	48.6	18.7	10.4	17.1	40.9	942	1,246	32.3
El Salvador	70.8	62.4	23.4	23.0	5.8	14.6	1,129	609	-46.1
Guatemala	58.5	55.3	25.1	22.0	16.4	22.7	1,221	1,073	-12.1
Honduras	63.7	64.2	7.9	2.9	28.4	32.9	757	893	18
Nicaragua	67.2	61.9	14.6	8.5	18.2	29.7	616	236	-61.7

a. Includes coffee, bananas, cotton, sugar and meat only. Other traditional products (different according to country) are included under "non-traditional."

Source: Consejo Monetario Centroamericano and PREALC, "El trasfondo politico-economico del fomento de las exportaciones no tradicionales en America Central: El ajuste estructural y sus efectos sociales," Ian Walker, 1992.

---

market structures and technologies, as illustrated in Figure 4. The growth of NTAEs in the 1980s and early 1990s has been supported by international financial agencies and bilateral development agencies, mainly the U.S. Agency for International Development (USAID). These institutions have required most developing countries to establish structural adjustment and trade- liberalization policies in attempts to reduce their external debt and open their economies to increased exports and investment. Structural adjustment generally consists of three kinds of policy prescriptions: (a) changes in currency valuation to establish competitive exchange rates; (b) commercial/trade liberalization policies to reduce tariffs and other trade restrictions; and (c) financial liberalization to encourage foreign investment.[47] Adjustment policies also require reducing the role of the state by, for example, privatizing public enterprises, cutting back government support for social and economic programs, and decreasing market regulations.[48]

From the perspectives of development agencies and governments, the purposes of NTAE-promotion policies and programs are to generate foreign exchange to repay debts, increase investments, reduce dependence on traditional exports, create jobs, and, in general, revitalize economic growth.[49] In Colombia and Bolivia, where narcotics production is prevalent, NTAEs are also seen as high-value alternatives to coca. Still other goals of the NTAE strategy are to fulfill the growing demands of northern consumers and to benefit northern companies. In some countries, such as Guatemala, "broad-based" development has been added to USAID's aims of NTAE promotion, suggesting an interest in increasing jobs and opportunities for small farmers.[50] However, whether these ambitious objectives are fulfilled in reality is a central question explored in this study.

Financial support of the NTAE strategy in Latin America comes mainly from USAID. *(See Table 3.)* Through the 1980s, the Agency created and supported many programs and institutions dedicated to NTAEs. For example, in fiscal year 1992, it spent nearly $119 million directly on agribusiness worldwide,[51] mostly on non-traditional crops. Additional funds were spent indirectly on NTAEs through various USAID programs on rural develop-

Figure 4. An Overview of Inducements and Impacts of NTAE Growth

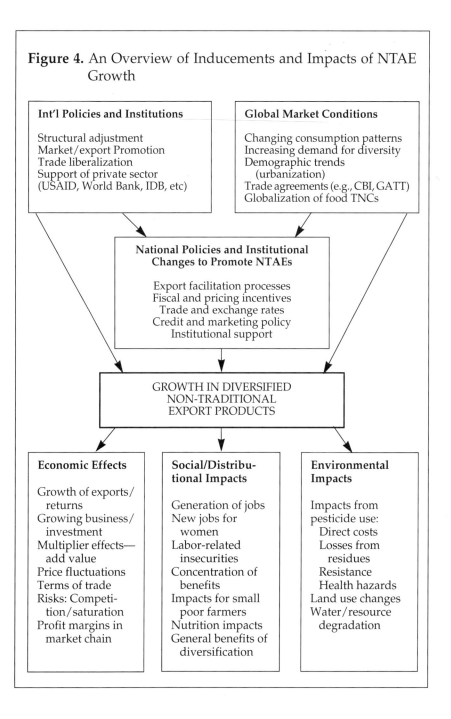

Table 3. NTAE-Related Projects Funded by USAID

Country/Project Title	Category[a]	Dates[b]	Total Budget ($US)
Belize			
Commercialization of Alternative Crops	1	1985–1990	6,800,000
Toledo Agricultural Marketing	1	1987–1992	2,500,000
Export Investment Promotion	2	1986–1991	3,000,000
Costa Rica			
Non-Traditional Export Technology Support	1	1986–1989	3,500,000
Private Agricultural and Agroindustrial Council	1	not available	not available
Private Investment Corporation	2	1984–1988	21,000,000
Agricultural and Industrial Reactivation	2	1986–1989	20,000,000
El Salvador			
Water Management	1	1985–1990	18,744,000
Agribusiness Development	1	1987–1992	20,000,000
Association Strengthening	2	1985–1989	1,945,000
Guatemala			
Agribusiness Development	1	1985–1990	12,500,000
Private Enterprise Development	2	1987–1992	10,000,000
Honduras			
Export Development and Services	1	1984–1989	23,500,000
Agricultural Research Foundation	2	1984–1994	20,000,000
Policy Analysis and Implementation	2	1987–1994	7,300,000
Central America Region			
Non-Traditional Agricultural Export Support	1	1985–1991	8,000,000
Export Agribusiness Development	1	1986–1989	15,000,000

Country/Project Title	Category[a]	Dates[b]	Total Budget ($US)
Dominican Republic			
Agricultural Promotion	1	1985–1988	19,800,000
Commercial Farming Systems	1	1987–1992	14,750,000
Agricultural Policy Analysis	2	1984–1988	500,000
Export and Investment Promotion	2	1985–1989	6,000,000
Development Training	2	1986–1991	7,000,000
Sugar Diversification	2	1987–1992	3,500,000
Jamaica			
Crop Diversification and Irrigation	2	1985–1990	18,000,000
Agricultural Research	2	1986–1993	7,600,000
Caribbean Region			
Caribbean Agricultural Trading Co.	1	1982–1988	1,695,000
High Impact Agricultural Marketing and Production	1	1986–1991	25,200,000
Caribbean Financial Services	2	not available	17,735,000
Eastern Caribbean Farming Systems R&D	2	1983–1988	755,000
Investment Promotion and Export Dev.	2	1984–1989	17,200,000
Ecuador			
Non-Traditional Agricultural Exports	1	1984–1988	10,400,000
Rural Technology Transfer Systems	2	1980–1988	10,300,000
Agricultural Sector Reorientation	2	1985–1990	8,500,000

a. 1 = directly related to crop diversification/NTAE
   2 = closely related to crop diversification/NTAE
b. authorization date through project activity completion date
Source: Stephen Lack (team leader), "Agricultural Crop Diversification/Export Promotion Cross-Cutting Evaluation," unpublished report, (Washington, D.C.: Experience, Inc. and USAID, 1989). I-13.

ment. The regional office in Central America (ROCAP), dedicated approximately $15.3 million dollars to the Export Promotion Project called PROEXAG from 1985 to 1992, as well as additional funds to banks to support credit and other activities to promote NTAE business.[52] Other USAID-sponsored non-traditional programs in Central America include the Project for Agricultural Diversification (PRODIVERSA) in Honduras, the Foundation for Salvadoran Development (FUSADES) in El Salvador, and CINDE in Costa Rica. Although development agencies provided relatively little financial support to early NTAE booms in Chile, Mexico, and Colombia, USAID's backing for the Chile Foundation in the 1970's became a model for later projects. In Ecuador, USAID provided $8 million from 1984 through 1988 for Phase 1 of the Program for the Export of Non-traditional Agriculture (PROEXANT), followed by $4.5 million in Phase 2 during 1989–1994.[53] These USAID-sponsored projects include a range of activities to build NTAE enterprises. In Guatemala, for example, USAID export promotion programs have supported the Association of Non-Traditional Exporters (GEXPRONT), large agricultural export companies such as ALCOSA (tied to Hanover Brands), and trade conventions. In Ecuador, PROEXANT's main activities are policy dialogue for export facilitation laws, communications services, trade conferences, market research, quality control, and technology transfer for pest control and other production practices. Many NTAE programs include aggressive advertising campaigns to attract investors. It is difficult to calculate the percentage of USAID's allocations to non-traditional exports because of overlaps in accounting records, but, as shown in Figure 5, funds for this sector are substantial compared to those for other sectors.[54]

International agencies, such as the Commonwealth Development Corporation (CDC), the World Bank, and the Inter-American Development Bank (IDB), also support policies for non-traditional agroexport growth, as well as for traditional exports.[55] In Ecuador, for example, the CDC dedicated $10 million to NTAE promotion, the IDB approved a $1-million loan for NTAEs, the German government provided technical assistance, and the Canadian government is providing support for NTAE transport.[56]

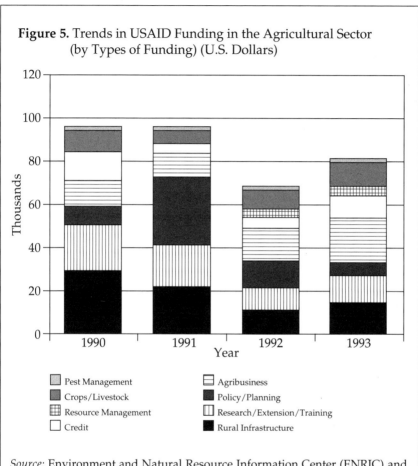

Figure 5. Trends in USAID Funding in the Agricultural Sector (by Types of Funding) (U.S. Dollars)

Source: Environment and Natural Resource Information Center (ENRIC) and Latin America and the Caribbean Rural Development Office, USAID, Washington, D.C. (unpublished data).

C. International Market Conditions and Trade Policies Influencing NTAEs

International market conditions and regional trade policies, coinciding with prevalent macroeconomic development policies, have also favored the growth of high-value export crops.

1. Consumption Trends

In industrial countries, consumers' increasing preferences for dietary diversity, and increased health consciousness are key demand-side factors favoring growing world trade and prices for these commodities.[57] Increasingly, northern consumers are shifting their diets away from grains and meats and toward fruits and vegetables.[58] In the United States, total vegetable consumption increased from an average of 73.2 pounds per person in 1974, to 85.6 pounds per person in 1987.[59] Market studies also show a growing preference for fresh produce over canned goods.[60]

The growth in demand has been particularly rapid for specialty fruits and vegetables—unusual products not available in temperate zones year-round. Between 1980 and 1986, this category of products grew at an annual rate of 13 percent, compared to a 2-percent growth rate for vegetables produced in the United States.[61] Similarly, demands for exotic specialty products have grown substantially in Europe.[62]

Increasing numbers of consumers who want to decrease health risks by lowering intake of fats and cholesterol realize that fruits and vegetables are a source of Vitamin C and fiber. But these same health-conscious consumers are increasingly concerned about pesticide residues and are demanding more organically grown or pesticide-free produce. In the United States, the largest distributor of organic foods, Organic Farms, doubled its sales to $22 million by 1988.[63] The organic market today is still a limited specialty market, but it is rapidly expanding and opens new opportunities for produce grown in many parts of the world.[64] *(See Chapter V.)*

Demographic changes in the North and South also favor the non-traditional food market. Urbanization has increased consumer demands for processed foods and for fresh produce. The growth of Hispanic, Asian, and African populations in both Europe and the United States helps drive rising consumption of diverse foods once considered "ethnic."[65] The increase in average incomes throughout industrial countries has also expanded demand: wealthier people can afford more expensive specialty fruits and vegetables.[66] As markets grow, the price decline of some of these products also boosts consumption.

Another significant global trend that has encouraged NTAE growth is the major decline in prices of traditional agricultural exports such as coffee, sugar, cotton, bananas, and basic grains in the 1980's.[67] The diminishing growth of traditional exports is tied to changes in consumer demand, as well as to saturation of markets for these products. The World Bank estimates for real price changes from 1989 to 1995 are -3.0 percent per year for cocoa, -0.5 percent for coffee, and - 5.0 percent for rice; and this descent is expected to continue.[68] Price declines have led to a fall in production and prompted producers to seek new markets and diverse products.

2. Supply and Marketing Conditions
On the supply side, innovations in products, production processes, and distribution systems, achieved mainly through investments of foreign capital and the increasing globalization of northern-based transnational agribusinesses, have favored growth and added value to the NTAE sector.[69] Investments in packaging, storage, and transportation are fueling increased diversification in support-service activities, such as long-distance cargo handling. The development of sophisticated capital-intensive "cool chains" for refrigeration from harvest site to market shelf illustrates how modern transport technology can help boost NTAEs.[70] Similarly, improvements in information systems and communication networks can help facilitate more efficient product movement. Increased advertising by commodity organizations and by transnational food corporations fuel NTAE growth too.

Tropical countries also provide conventional conditions of "comparative advantage" for NTAEs: very low labor and land rent costs compared to Northern countries, more lenient environmental regulations, and favorable climatic and soil conditions that permit year-round production. These factors attract foreign investors and can also benefit local producers.[71] For some products, such as tomatoes in Mexico, a strong domestic market has favored the subsequent growth of an export industry.[72]

3. Trade Agreements and Regional Policies
International and regional trade agreements and policies have influenced export expansion as well. In particular, the Caribbean

Basin Initiative (CBI) established in 1983, the Generalized System of Preferences (GSP) of 1976, and the Andean Trade Preference Act (ATPA) passed in 1991, provide influential trade incentives.[73] They allow products to enter the U.S. market duty-free or under reduced tariffs.[74] The GSP, for example, "provides preferential duty-free entry to approximately 4,284 products from 134 designated beneficiary countries and territories... The objective is to help [developing] countries to compete better in U.S. markets and to diversify their economic structures away from production of primary goods."[75] Similarly, the CBI created a union of Central American and Caribbean nations "designed to encourage development of the Caribbean Basin principally by authorizing certain U.S. nonreciprocal preferential trade benefits for the CB countries and territories."[76] Its main aim was to improve the economic performance of the region and, particularly, to revitalize export-led development.[77] The CBI also established incentives for foreign investment. The Andean Trade Preference Act, modelled after CBI legislation, extended trade preferences to the Andean region.[78]

The provisions of the North American Free Trade Agreement (NAFTA) and the General Agreement on Tariffs and Trade (GATT) encourage export expansion of agricultural products (and exports in general) mainly by reducing trade barriers that were in place before the trade negotiations of the 1990s.[79] Under GATT provisions, fruits and vegetables generally have less restrictive tariff barriers than mass-consumed food commodities, such as grains. GATT also mandates the use of sanitary and phytosanitary regulations and other quality standards that are established through the World Health Organization and other international bodies; and these standards constitute non-tariff trade barriers for many of the export products.[80] It is not clear how current NAFTA and GATT conditions will specifically affect NTAE sectors, but in general the agreements are inducing agroexport growth and contributing to a climate of trade deregulation and liberalization.

While NTAE products are covered by general provisions of GSP and GATT, the United States and other importing countries have also established their own market policies affecting these imported commodities, ranging from quotas for quantities to regulations on sanitary qualities and pesticide residues. Some national

28

import policies supersede these broad trade agreements and have significant impacts on the NTAE sector, as discussed below.

D. National Policy Changes Influencing NTAE Growth

During the 1980s and 1990s, developing countries adhering to the policies and structural adjustment conditions mandated by international agencies have established policy reforms and institutional support mechanisms favorable to NTAEs. These reforms include export-facilitation procedures, trade and exchange rate policies, subsidies and fiscal modifications, and agricultural credit and marketing policies. Generally, these changes have emerged as a part of broader national policy reform programs for structural adjustment intended to stabilize exchange rates, lower deficits, and stimulate growth.[81]

1. Export-Facilitation Procedures

One of the most common and effective policy mechanisms used to support the NTAE sector is the development of export-facilitation procedures. Before the emergence of NTAE promotion, most developing countries required all exporters to go through a complex legal and administrative obstacle course administered by several state institutions. In Ecuador, for example, before the 1990s, exporters had to fill out 40 forms and submit multiple copies, obtain up to 254 signatures, acquire legal permits from several agencies, and comply with several inspection processes—all of which took an average of 138 hours per shipment.[82] In Mexico, over fifty separate government agency approvals were required to set up an export-oriented industry.[83] This red tape added costs that were often crippling, if not prohibitive, for export businesses. New export strategies, following the recommendations of development agencies, have substantially reduced and simplified these complex procedures.[84] Starting in the mid-1980s, most countries have introduced a "one-stop window" (*ventanilla unica*) as the main single administrative unit to facilitate export procedures, thereby reducing the requirements and streamlining the inspections, permit processes, and paperwork. In Ecuador, for example, a one-stop window was established in 1992 in the Central Bank, as a result of the Export Facilitation Law.

29

2. Exchange Rates and Fiscal Policies

Low or moderate inflation and flexible stable exchange rates have been identified as macroeconomic policy factors that contribute to NTAE growth.[85] According to some analysts, an appropriate exchange rate policy is one of the most important conditions determining the competitiveness and growth of exports.[86] During the 1970s and 1980s, however, most Latin American governments had overvalued and unstable exchange rates, high rates of inflation, and generally high taxes on imported inputs, all of which constrained productivity and trade. In the 1990s, governments have established policy measures to change such macroeconomic conditions.[87]

From 1986 to 1990, for example, the Guatemalan government tried to control fluctuating exchange rates by unifying the multiple exchange rate markets under one system.[88] However, these efforts initially backfired, elevating inflation and exacerbating economic problems for local people.[89] In 1991, the newly elected government stabilized these conditions, bringing inflation down to 10 percent, lowering interest rates, and stabilizing exchange rates to some extent.[90] Ecuador's government has also tried to reduce the instability of the exchange rates typical in the 1980s through policy reforms, and since 1992, these rates have become more favorable to exporters.

Following advice from USAID and the World Bank, most governments have also established tax policy changes intended to stimulate NTAE growth. In Colombia, for example, the government established a special kind of tax credit certificate known as a *Certificado de Abono Tributario* (CAT), which could be used to pay most taxes (and not just offset income tax liability). Colombia's export program also subsidized loans for flowers.[91] In Costa Rica, during the 1980's, the CAT was also used as the main fiscal incentive for NTAEs. Although this export tax credit was phased out in the early 1990s, Costa Rica provides other policy incentives to promote diverse agroexports and other products. *(See Box 2.)*

Following mandates for structural adjustment and market liberalization in Latin America, most governments decreased or eliminated taxes and policies that discouraged export activities.[92] For example, most of the governments in the region now allow duty-free imports for inputs such as chemicals used in export production, and they do not levy taxes on non-traditional exports.[93] In some cases, as in Ecuador, the government has not established explicit subsidies, but has created other kinds of programs to promote this sector. Such fiscal policies have generally contributed to an economic environment conducive to export growth.

3. Credit and Marketing Capacities

Credit is an essential element for increasing export production.[94] Historically, most agricultural loans in Latin America were granted mainly to large enterprises for traditional export production.[95] However, during the 1980s, some governments, assisted by international financial agencies, increased the credit available for non-traditional crops through central or commercial banks.[96] In Guatemala, for example, loans for non-traditional export vegetables and fruits grew at a rate of 18 and 67 percent, respectively, between 1986 and 1990; by 1990, fruits received the second largest share of loans, next to coffee.[97] In Ecuador, credit for NTAEs was available in the late 1980s and early 1990s through the National Finance Corporation (CFN), financed mainly by loans from the World Bank, Interamerican Development Bank (IDB), USAID, and Corporación Andina Financiera.[98] Most of this credit has been directed to large well-established entrepreneurs.[99] In the 1990s, however, credit has become increasingly limited across all sectors throughout the developing world because of restrictions from international and public lending institutions. Credit is still available for some NTAE enterprises, but accessibility has declined. Poor farmers suffer more severely from such restricted access to credit.

Policies and programs have also been developed to improve crucial infrastructure, marketing, and transport capacities for NTAEs. Although the private sector is mainly responsible for developing these kinds of capacities, governments in Latin America have also supported market promotion, through activities such as publicity campaigns, trade fairs, quality control, and support of trading companies.

4. Institutional Support

Throughout Latin America a variety of government agencies, including Ministries of Commerce and Industry, Ministries of

31

Box 2. Policy Factors Shaping NTAE Growth in Costa Rica

Costa Rica has established several strong fiscal incentives to promote the non-traditional agroexport sector. These policy incentives have been established as part of a broader aggressive strategy to open markets and to attract foreign investment. The main fiscal incentive established for non-traditional exporters was the Certificado de Abono Tributario (CAT)—a special tax credit. CATs were originally awarded to firms exporting non-traditional commodities, with the provision that the exports must have a minimum of 35 percent national value-added. The CAT was up to 20 percent of the value of a firm's NTAEs, and was negotiable on the Costa Rican stock exchange. CATs were used as a basis for financing many investments in NTAEs during the late 1980s. The CAT expenditures were 19 times greater in 1989 than in 1984, and by 1990 were expected to account for 8 percent of the government's budget.

The CAT was phased out in the early 1990s in Costa Rica, however, mainly because the subsidy was becoming too costly for the government and some industries became overdependent on it. In addition, a detailed investigation revealed that the CATs were unfairly concentrated in the hands of a small number of

Agriculture, national banks, and planning agencies, as well as private organizations, have supported NTAE growth and policies.

In Ecuador, for example, the National Finance Corporation not only provides credit for NTAE producers, but also gives technical assistance to creditors, carries out marketing research and feasibility studies on crops, and helps formulate export laws. The Ministry of Industry and Commerce offers training on product quality and market standards, disseminates market information, and participates actively in trade fairs to promote NTAEs. In Guatemala, the state helps support NTAEs by contributing to the Agricultural Development Program and the National Agricultural Reorganization/Irrigation Program, both of which include components to in-

---

Box 2. (continued)

large companies. Eight companies alone gained 27 percent of all CATs in one 18-month period in the late 1980s. Moreover, corrupt practices (mainly over-invoicing) were being used by some companies to gain additional CATs. At the same time, suspension of this policy was also recommended by the World Bank. Even though the CAT was rescinded, Costa Rica has established other incentives for NTAEs, particularly the following:
- 100 percent exemption for NTAE businesses on import duties for raw materials and capital goods, export taxes, municipal and capital taxes, local sales and excise taxes, and profit repatriation taxes;
- training support on NTAE production and marketing provided to growers by the government's export program;
- simple capital and profit-repatriation regulations; and
- free trade zones for special investment opportunities.

Source: Clark, Mary. 1992, "Costa Rica's Export Strategy," *Hemisphere*, Summer, p. 10; CINDE, 1993, Export Promotion information, San José: Costa Rican Investment and Development; Mary Clark, personal communication, October 1994.

---

crease NTAE production. In recent years, the plant protection divisions of the Ministries of Agriculture have also developed technical assistance projects to address pest control and pesticide residue monitoring in NTAEs, mainly in response to emerging residue problems.

Private organizations and trade associations are playing increasingly important roles as well. In Ecuador, for example, such trade associations as the Federation of Exporters (FEDEXPOR) and the Flower Growers Guild (EXPOFLORES), support NTAE interests. In Guatemala, the Association of Exporters of Non-traditional Products (GEXPRONT), with state support, backs export policies such as the National Plan for NTAE Promotion, and provides its

members with information on trade, marketing, and technical assistance. Typically, such private institutions, as well as USAID's
promotion programs, serve mostly large capitalized producers,
while the special needs of small-scale, poorer farmers are not so
well served. The latter tend to have limited access to services, information, and marketing connections.

Currently, institutional support from both the state and USAID
to NTAE programs is declining in the face of funding constraints.
Consequently, many institutional services for exports are being privatized, resulting in new challenges for producers and exporters,
especially smaller farmers, to sustain NTAE business.

E. Environmental and Socioeconomic Policy
   Considerations

Independent of these economic policies, environmental initiatives
are being developed to alleviate the degradation of natural resources in the region. Government and nongovernment institutions
in Latin America, encouraged by international agencies, have
begun to establish environmental policies and programs.[100] In the
agricultural arena, these efforts often entail technical projects such
as soil conservation, integrated pest management (IPM), agroforestry, and use of green manures. Sometimes, broader policies on,
for example, pesticides, deforestation, and land use are established.

But environmental policies and programs generally have relatively little influence over agroexport sectors, either traditional or
non-traditional. In general, concerns about environmental sustainability and natural resources are poorly integrated into economic
growth policies. Decision-makers and institutions supporting environmental policies have rarely interacted or collaborated with
agribusiness; each generally works separately under independent,
and often conflicting, mandates. Even *within* such institutions as
USAID, the World Bank, and national agricultural ministries and
research programs, the departments for environment and for
agribusiness are usually separate, and environmental policies
often are secondary concerns.

Although pesticide regulations exist as written documents
throughout most of Latin American, they are not adequately

implemented for NTAEs and other crops.[101] Few government agencies have the resources or the political will needed to enforce the laws. Furthermore, most countries have contradictory policy incentives for pesticides such as subsidies and credit policies that encourage heavy use of agrochemicals in export crops.[102]

In the planning and initial stages of NTAE programs, most decision-makers and administrators paid little attention to environmental issues, such as pesticide use, land use changes, and water quality. Indeed, they were often ambivalent or even antagonistic toward such concerns. Although environmental impact reviews were required by law at the outset for USAID's export-promotion programs, these assessments were usually conducted after the programs were firmly established with approved financing.[103] Moreover, although some assessments identified likely problems and suggested measures to avoid them, their recommendations were rarely implemented in the first years of the NTAE programs.

Decision-makers concerned with NTAEs tend to perceive environmental reviews and recommendations as bureaucratic burdens, sometimes scorning organic farming as well. In Guatemala, for example, NTAE promotion officers openly opposed the development of organic NTAE products and markets for many years, until they finally witnessed in 1994 that organic agribusiness could be lucrative and successful.[104] Investors and administrators behind NTAE policies have focussed on maximizing growth and export earnings, responding to the immediate imperatives imposed by international finance agencies, consumers, and distributors, rather than addressing the broader social and environmental concerns.

As an exception, the regulation of pesticide residues in imported foods does significantly influence agroexports. Regulations are set by importing countries—for instance, the Environmental Protection Agency (EPA) and the Food and Drug Administration (FDA) in the United States. The safeguards established by the FDA and EPA state that "raw products are illegal if they contain residues of pesticides not authorized by, or in excess of, tolerances established by EPA regulations," according to the Federal Food, Drug, and Cosmetic Act.[105] These tolerance standards, based on detailed analyses, are established to reduce consumers' risk of cancer or other health problems.[106] In response, several countries including

Ecuador, Guatemala, Costa Rica, and Chile, have established programs to address pesticide residues in NTAEs, but only *after* the
emergence of serious problems with violations *(see Chapter 4)*.

Like environmental impacts, the social dimensions of NTAEs—
i.e., equity in distributional impacts, fairness of labor conditions,
and effects on poor farmers' livelihoods—have received relatively
little attention in NTAE policies and programs. The emphasis of
such programs is generally on commercial goals and business capacities. According to a recent USAID evaluation of Ecuador's
NTAE project, "interest in producer cooperatives…, small farmers
and contract farming was not a high priority [from 1984 until the
early 1990s]…and the types of enterprises which emerged did not
concentrate on employment generation and participation by disadvantaged groups."[107] Yet, in a few situations, as in Guatemala,
NTAE policies and USAID-supported programs were initiated at
least partly to benefit poor farmers and to generate jobs through assistance to cooperatives.[108] In the 1990s, as small-farmer associations, research analysts, and the media have revealed these social
questions, NTAE policy-makers and USAID programs in other
Latin American countries have also been paying more heed to
socioeconomic impacts and supporting new opportunities for
small farmers.

In sum, the strong policy incentives for maximizing the short-
term growth of export earnings and market competition, along
with relative inattention to social and environmental concerns,
contrast with the emergent policy rhetoric for sustainable human
development. Such political-economic conditions are important in-
fluences on the socioeconomic and environmental outcomes.

III.
A PROFILE OF CURRENT AGROEXPORT SYSTEMS

The term "non-traditional agricultural export products" covers such a large variety of products that it is somewhat difficult to make sweeping generalizations about the NTAE sector. Nonetheless, high-value fruits, vegetables, and flowers share several general common characteristics that influence the impacts and sustainability of production.

A. General Characteristics of NTAE Production and Marketing

The systems of production and marketing for NTAEs have several general production characteristics. A few are distinct from those of traditional export systems; but others are similar.[109] *(See Box 3.)* One of the most significant features that is unique to NTAE commodities is their relatively high unit value. In recent years, many NTAE fresh fruit and vegetable products have international prices of $500 or more per metric ton, while traditional crops of sorghum, maize and wheat have ranged from $75 to $175 per metric ton.[110] At such high prices, the main market of many NTAEs is the middle- and upper-income consumers. A second feature is that fresh NTAE products are highly perishable and have shorter shelf-lives than many traditional products so investor risks are higher; specialized production and packaging technologies as well as modern and refrigerated transport systems are essential. Third, NTAEs require highly sophisticated and well-integrated marketing networks, accompanied by complex information systems and new global structures for transport and distribution in "food commodity systems," often via transnational corporations. Fourth, NTAEs

Box 3. A Summary of Characteristics of Non-traditional
Agricultural Export Systems

Unique Features (different from traditional exports):
• Very high prices and values (per unit of land) for NTAE
products;
• High perishability for most products, requiring specialized
technologies and transport;
• Complex marketing networks and interlinked food com-
modity systems;
• Farms of various sizes, from large plantations to small plots.
Features similar to traditional export systems:
• Intense competition among producers in international markets;
• High capital investment and high operating costs, with close
links to foreign capital;
• Monocultures of standard crop varieties and production
methods within each farm;
• Dependence on high inputs of imported technology, especially heavy use of pesticides;
• Division of labor, with centralized management and dependency on low-wage local laborers;
• Heavy stress on speed of production processes and maximization of short-term returns.
• Requirements to fulfill strict marketing demands of Northern
importers, including:
 high quality and uniformity of products, with aesthetic
 criteria for "perfect" appearance;
 tight restrictions on export time periods ("windows");
 stringent phytosanitary and sanitary standards;
 regulations on pesticide residues in food imports.

Sources: Field observations and interviews with production managers
and workers in Ecuador and Guatemala, 1993. Also see, e.g.,
Kaimowitz, David. 1992. *El apoyo tecnológico necesario para promover las
exportaciones agrícolas notradicionales en American Central.* no. 30. San
José, Costa Rica: IICA; Jaffee, Steven. 1993. *Exporting High-Value Food
Commodities: Success Stories from Developing Countries.* World Bank
Discussion Paper, Number 198. Washington, D.C.: World Bank.

are produced on farms of varying sizes, ranging from small plots to large plantations.

On the other hand, certain NTAE features are very similar to those of traditional agroexport plantation and marketing systems. These enterprises face intense competition in international markets and require high levels of capital investment and high operating costs. NTAE products are generally planted in monocultures that depend on high inputs of imported technology, especially pesticides. Most production systems involve strict division of labor, with centralized management and unspecialized low-wage local laborers, and stress speedy processes and the maximization of short-term returns. Finally, NTAEs must comply with the requirements of importers, especially the demand for blemish-free produce, tight restrictions on when products can be exported (intended to protect northern producers), stringent phytosanitary and sanitary standards, and regulations on pesticide residues in food products.

Many features of NTAEs are illustrated by cut-flower production in Ecuador. *(See Box 4.)* Although these flower plantations are usually small in area, they require very high capital investment (an average initial investment of $200,000 per hectare), highly complex technology and marketing, and compliance with stringent market demands.

Almost all of the features of NTAEs contrast sharply with crops for subsistence or for local markets. Staple production for subsistence purposes usually entails comparatively little capital, low (or no) chemical inputs, polycultural small-scale systems, no influence of foreign standards, and heavy reliance on family labor. Crops for local consumption also have comparatively low unit value, require less complex or no marketing transactions, and are generally less perishable. These common differences are among the many factors that make it hard for poor farmers to enter and compete in the NTAE market.

B. Import Requirements and the Demand-Driven Character of NTAEs

NTAEs are demand-driven, and thus highly dependent on economic conditions in other countries.[111] Market requirements largely deter-

Box 4. Features of Flower Production in Ecuador

From 1985 to October 1991, flower production in Ecuador grew by 1,522 percent (15-fold) in volume and 3,055 percent in value. Between 1990 and 1992 alone, the number of producers doubled, reaching about 70. This remarkable boom stems from several factors, especially the high value of the product, technical changes, an increase in the varieties of flowers demanded and exported, access to foreign capital, and such baseline conditions as an excellent climate for flowers and the availability of inexpensive labor.

A 1991 survey indicated that 45 percent of the flower firms received some foreign investment, and 75 percent work with foreign brokers. Although most plantations were founded by Ecuadorians, foreign investors—in many cases Colombian flower producers looking for secure investment alternatives—have entered the sector. Two out of three investors are from urban areas. Virtually all firms export 90 percent or more of their production, mostly to the United States, but also to Western Europe, Canada, and Japan.

The flower industry in Ecuador is concentrated in the highland region, near Quito and the airport. Plantations have sophisticated infrastructure, including complex irrigation and drainage systems and electric lights for night lighting. Flowers are grown in plastic-covered greenhouses, and the beds are prepared with many soil supplements. Post-harvest handling, sorting, packaging, and loading takes place in buildings with sophisticated cooling systems. Flower production is systematically planned, timed, and executed to meet quality standards and other market demands. Exports peak during special holidays in North America—particularly Valentine's Day and Mothers' Day.

These plantations depend on imported inputs. Chemical fertilizers and pesticides are applied heavily and frequently, on

Box 4. (continued)

a calendar basis by laborers. Unlike food products, flowers are *not* inspected for pesticide residues by importers, so producers have relatively little concern about residues. The environment within the greenhouses is artificial and chemically "sanitized." The aim is to control all variables. Many producers hire specialists in floriculture from Holland, Colombia, and other foreign countries to manage their farms. If quality or timing is not right, high financial losses ensue.

The 1990 survey also showed that the average flower plantation in Ecuador is only about seven hectares, even though the investment per hectare was very large. Flower production is extremely labor intensive; the worker to area ratio is 15.4 per hectare. Of 5,058 workers surveyed, 3,149 (62 percent) were women. Many of the flower businesses offer medical services, lunch, and transportation to their workers.

The initial installation and preparation of greenhouses and fields for flowers involves many months and a remarkably large capital investment, estimated at an average of $200,000 per hectare. Annual input costs are also high, especially for agrochemicals. A feasibility study carried out in 1989 by a rose entrepreneur reports that nine fertilizers, six fungicides, and four insecticides are applied regularly for rose production. In the first full year of production, this firm planned to spend $18,913 on agrochemicals, at a cost per hectare of $9,306 for fertilizers, $1,233 for fungicides, and $2,780 for insecticides.

Source: William F. Waters. "Restructuring of Ecuadorian Agriculture and the Development of Nontraditional Exports: Evidence from the Cut Flower Industry." Paper presented at the 55th Meeting of the Rural Sociological Society. University Park, Pennsylvania. (Quito: Universidad San Francisco de Quito, 1992.)

mine the production and marketing practices of NTAE enterprises. This is also true of traditional exports, but importers' demands and consumer preferences affecting NTAEs are even more stringent, detailed, and influential on the patterns and impacts of production. NTAE producers must comply first with buyers' quality standards, including detailed criteria for shape, size, ripeness, color, and taste. Second, they must comply with regulations for permits and licenses, inspections, and documentation in both exporting and importing countries. Although export procedures have been simplified, exporters must also pass through a gamut of regulatory procedures in the importing country. In the United States, for example, they must acquire customs permits, pass phytosanitary and sanitary inspections and pesticide residue tests, comply with special quality standards called "marketing orders," and sometimes pay buyers' fees.[112] The U.S. government also sets quotas on Latin American exports of frozen orange juice, asparagus, broccoli, carrots, and cantaloupes. These products are allowed entry only through specified import windows—that is, at certain places and time periods—to protect U.S. producers from competition.[113] (National regulations usually override broad GATT provisions.) NTAE products such as frozen produce and canned goods are subject to less strict quality standards and import procedures, but requirements are still demanding.

In the United States, all shipments must be screened by federal regulatory agencies, as indicated in Figure 6, including the Food and Drug Administration (FDA), the U.S. Department of Agriculture (USDA), the Animal and Plant Health Inspection Service (APHIS), and the U.S. Environmental Protection Agency (EPA).[114] Exporters and brokers must also fill out numerous forms, including commercial invoices, airway bills, delivery certificates, product quality papers for the FDA, and bonds for any shipment over $1,000.[115] Inspectors from the FDA undertake random testing of pesticide residues in samples of all fresh imports. About one percent of all imports of fresh produce are tested. Shipments that do not comply with all regulations are subject to detention; they must be brought into compliance, destroyed, or re-exported.[116] If detentions are frequent, the FDA can temporarily place an "automatic" detention on a product, meaning that it must be tested in the coun-

Figure 6. Production Challenges for an Exporter of Non-traditional Agroexport Crops

Main Types of Challenges in Latin America

Developing Market Opportunities (Market Research Links with Buyers)

Packing and Transport (Post Harvest Management)

Credit and Finances

Export Laws/Processes (e.g. taxes, permits, customs)

Production Challenges (e.g. Pests, Climate, Pesticide Use, Soils)

Fulfill Market Demand, Quality and Timing, Residue Standards

Import Requirements and Regulators in the U.S.*
An Exported Product must pass through:

U.S. Customs Service
Collects taxes on imports and statistics on trade/commerce; prevents contraband

APHIS—Animal Plant Health Inspection Service
Regulates fresh products, plants and plant products, animals and animal products

Food Safety Inspection Service (in USDA)
Regulates meat and poultry; certifies packing facilities

Agricultural Marketing Service (in USDA)
Applies "market orders," regulates grading standards and aesthetic standards

Food and Drug Administration (FDA)
Applies EPA laws on pesticide tolerances, regulates fresh and processed products for contaminants

This information is adapted from a figure by Robert Bailey, LACTECH, Chemonics, Washington, D.C.

try of origin before export. The sampling frequency is increased for crops that previously violated standards, and the added costs are charged to the exporter.

For NTAE enterprises and potential investors, some of these requirements present opportunities for technological change. However, they put heavy pressures on producers to deal with the vagaries of distant markets far beyond their control. In particular, complying with these demands taxes smaller firms, many of which lack the necessary capital and market information.

C. Product Types and Production Areas and Scale

Certain products have stood out as leaders in growth rate and value among the NTAEs—for example, flowers in Ecuador and Colombia, grapes and citrus in Chile, melons, snow peas, and broccoli in Guatemala, and flowers, ornamental plants, and pineapples in Costa Rica. In many cases, products have taken the lead partly because they were prioritized by export-promotion programs, generally on the basis of market studies of demand, and local climatic conditions.[117]

Many NTAE crops are temperate varieties new to the regions where they are now planted. Many local producers had no prior experience growing and marketing them. Transferred from foreign agroecosystems, these kinds of crops require foreign seeds and unfamiliar technologies, so they entail new challenges and greater entry barriers, especially for poor producers. Only in a few exceptional cases are the new agroexports indigenous foods such as *quinoa,* peach palm (*pejibaye*), and *araza*—products with more potential benefit for small-scale poorer farmers.

Geographically, NTAE farms are usually located close to major seaports or capital cities with airports and marketing facilities.[118] If production sites are beyond two or three hours travel time from the ports, transportation costs soar and crops can perish. Location of farms also depends partly on the agroecological and climatic requirements of the crop. For example, flower plantations in Ecuador are mostly located at high elevations, where the sunlight is intense and temperatures are optimal for flower production. In Guatemala, vegetables for export are concentrated in the highlands

44

outside of Guatemala City, where the soils, climate, and altitudes are well-suited for such crops.

Accurate data on total areas devoted to NTAEs is lacking; estimates for Central America and Ecuador are shown in Tables 4 and 5. The NTAE area makes up a relatively small proportion of total agricultural land, especially in Panama and Ecuador.[119] However, as previously stated, the values and net returns per hectare, as well as growth rates, are high.

NTAE farms range in size, from very small plots (less than a hectare) to immense plantations. In Honduras and Paraguay, very large plantations dominate.[120] In Guatemala, on the other hand, certain NTAE crops such as vegetables, are grown on small-scale

Table 4. Area Planted in NTAEs: Central America and Ecuador* (in hectares)

	Area cultivated for NTAEs	Distribution
Costa Rica	43,372	22.0
El Salvador	18,907	9.6
Guatemala	71,227	36.1
Honduras	24,145	12.2
Nicaragua	37,644	19.1
Panama	1,991	1.0
Ecuador	9,483	n.a.

* Central America figures are from 1990. Ecuador figure is from 1992.

Source: Andres Achong, "Alcances y limitaciones de las exportaciones agricolas no tradicionales," in Ana Beatriz Mendizábal P. and Jürgen Weller, eds., *Promesa o Espejismo?* (Panama City, Panama: Programa Regional del Empleo para America Latina y el Caribe, 1992) 397.

Table 5. Types of NTAEs in Area, Value, and Income in Central America, 1989

	Area (hectares) [1]	Distribution (%) [2]	Export FOB (million US$) [3]	Gross Income ($/ha) [3]/[1]
Fruits	31,314	15.7	102.5	3,273.30
Legumes	9,177	4.6	28.8	3,083.80
Nuts	10,073	5.0	4.6	456.67
Spices	3,957	2.0	2.0	505.43
Roots	5,284	2.6	16.8	3,179.41
Flowers and orn.	3,824	1.9	61.2	16,004.18
Tobacco	n.d.	n.d.	21.7	n.d.
Natural rubber	26,410	13.2	8.1	360.70
Others	109,734	54.9	49.7	452.91
Total	199,773	100.0	294.9	1,476.18

Source: Andres Achong, "Alcances y limitaciones de las exportaciones agricolas no tradicionales," in Ana Beatriz Mendizábal P. and Jürgen Weller, eds., *Promesa o Espejismo?* (Panama City, Panama: Programa Regional del Empleo para America Latina y el Caribe, 1992), 397.

farms. The average size of snow pea farms in the Guatemalan highlands, for example, generally ranges from 0.5 to 3 hectares.[121] In sharp contrast, most traditional export farming, except for coffee, is large-scale. Nonetheless, in some countries, NTAE land has, over time, become concentrated in the hands of a few *(see Chapter 4)*.[122]

D. Complex Food Commodity Systems

Production and marketing of NTAEs are linked in a network of exchange relations known as "food commodity systems."[123] *(See Figure 7.)* NTAE marketing systems cross country boundaries; at each stage, value is added as food products change hands or as they are graded, stored, packaged, processed, and transported. To function efficiently, such systems require timely and adequate use of sophisticated technical skills and assets. A division of labor is useful; and all of these activities need to be effectively coordinated. Organizational capacities and advanced communication systems are therefore indispensable to NTAE businesses.[124] NTAE commodity systems generally involve highly dependent marketing relations among producers, exporters, and intermediary brokers,[125] and they sometimes entail contract farming arrangements.[126] Such features are found in traditional export systems as well, but they tend to be more intricate and demanding for NTAEs. Again, becoming part of this complex system can be difficult, especially for poor producers.

E. Use of Resources and Pesticides in NTAEs

As in traditional agroexport systems, NTAE production relies on simplification, standardization, and control of natural resources.[127] To maximize yields, increase efficiency, and mitigate natural variables such as climate change, producers usually make heavy use of imported technologies, including uniform seed stocks, agrochemicals, and soil nutrient supplements. NTAE producers also cultivate the land continuously and intensively over several years in single crops. Flowers and some vegetables are grown in climate-controlled greenhouses, complete with electric lighting systems for the night. All efforts are directed toward meeting stringent market requirements. As noted by Cornell University analysts Merwin and Pritts (1993), "[these] aspects of current intensive production and marketing systems are probably not sustainable in their present form, but they have been developed in response to intensifying market conditions and pressures for higher short-term profitability."[128]

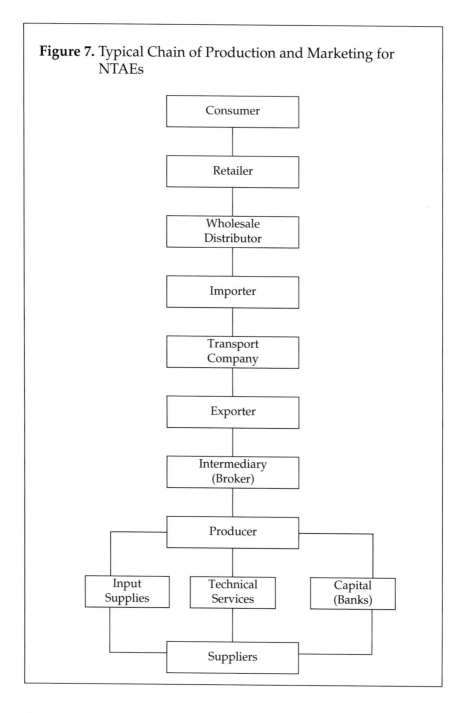

Figure 7. Typical Chain of Production and Marketing for NTAEs

Reacting to these pressures, producers typically apply large amounts of chemical pesticides. Generally, NTAE farms, like traditional export farms, are highly susceptible to pests and diseases partly because they are typically planted in monocultures, rather than in diverse polycultures. When the same crop is grown season after season, pest incidence is usually aggravated. Furthermore, many of the crops that come from temperate zones—for example, broccoli, strawberries, and asparagus—are more vulnerable to pests and diseases when transferred to the tropics. Not surprisingly, pest problems, including insects, nematodes, weeds, and diseases, have constrained production on numerous NTAE farms.[129]

Studies have shown consistently that all kinds of pesticides, including fungicides (for disease control), insecticides (for insects), nematicides (for nematodes), and herbicides (for weeds), are used more intensively for most high-value NTAEs than for other crops.[130] Pesticide applications per unit of land in NTAEs exceed those used on subsistence crops and crops sold in local markets and are similar or even greater per hectare than in many of the traditional export crops, such as coffee and sugarcane. Within the NTAE sector, the amounts of pesticides applied are particularly high for perishable fresh fruits, vegetables, and flowers. *(See Box 5.)*

Producers' decisions to use pesticides liberally cannot be seen as merely a "natural" reaction to high pest incidence; the following factors, depicted in Figure 8, are also influential:[131]

- Market requirements set by importers and Northern governments, particularly quality standards for size and aesthetic "perfection," obligations to maximize yields, and phytosanitary rules, impose pressures on exporters;
- In turn, national government policies in exporting countries promote compliance to importers' requirements by creating incentives, such as tax exemptions, that encourage the use of pesticides and other chemical inputs;
- The credit policies of both governments and exporting companies often require the use of specified standardized chemical applications (seen as "insurance") and other technologies as conditions for loans;

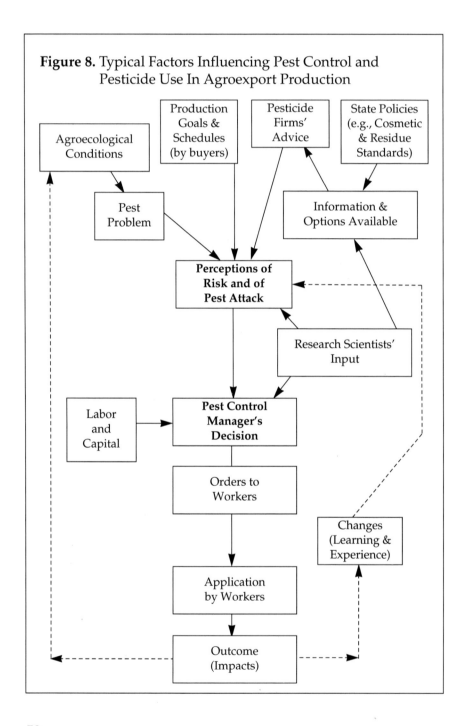

Figure 8. Typical Factors Influencing Pest Control and Pesticide Use In Agroexport Production

- Pesticide and fertilizer companies, actively soliciting throughout Latin America, encourage high chemical inputs through advertising and other promotion and the advice given out by their sales agents (who are usually paid on commission);
- Agroexport intermediaries (brokers), who frequently provide technical advice to their contract farmers, promote and often sell agrochemicals; and
- In turn, producers, under pressure to maximize quality and quantity, often have inflated perceptions of risks from pests, and feel compelled to do everything possible to ensure that their crops are not rejected by buyers.

In sum, farmers and other actors in the commodity systems generally perceive pesticide use as the best way to avoid risks and to ensure the quality consumers demand. Most adopt prophylactic schedules and believe that "more is better"—a misperception provoked partly by biased information sources. Surveys undertaken in Guatemala, Ecuador, and Costa Rica show that the large majority of farmers lack adequate information and technology for rational pesticide use or non-chemical alternative pest control methods. *(See Box 5.)*

On the other hand, pesticide-residue standards set by importing countries can influence chemical use patterns, since they raise consciousness about potential losses from violations. In many cases, standards have forced producers to be more judicious about the amounts and types of pesticides they apply. Yet, farmers are caught in a difficult bind—pressured by external agencies to reduce residues while simultaneously pushed to use more agrochemicals for esthetic and sanitary requirements. The immediate pressures to increase pesticide use tend to outweigh other considerations. Furthermore, the increasing attention to residues in exported foods is rarely accompanied by policies controlling residues in *locally* consumed foods and in the environment, and regulations to protect workers' health are still lacking.

In some limited cases, NTAE production can manage to avoid the pesticide treadmill. For instance, crops produced for canning or processing, such as industrial-grade tomatoes for making tomato

Box 5. Examples of Pesticide Use Patterns in NTAEs

Common patterns of pesticide use in NTAEs have been re-vealed in recent field studies undertaken by local investigators in collaboration with the World Resources Institute. In Ecuador, a 1992 survey of 54 growers and 104 workers revealed that producers consistently applied high volumes of pesticides to most NTAE crops. The survey found that 63 percent of the growers spray chemicals prophylactically, before pest out-breaks occur. In contrast, only 22 percent spray once the pest appears. Moreover, pesticides are applied very frequently: 29 percent of the growers applied them 16 to 20 days per month, and the rest between 5 and 15 days per month.

To determine methods of pesticide use, most growers in Ecuador rely on instructions from pesticide salespeople or product labels. Training on pesticide precautions has been min-imal, although some training was begun by PROEXANT as of 1993. Among the managers interviewed in 1992, 28 percent had received no training in pesticide use, 18 percent learned from pesticide salespeople, 29 percent learned from the distributors or buyers, 11 percent learned from private institutions, and 16 percent from state institutions. Most knew about phytosanitary requirements for their crops and used chemicals to keep prod-ucts pest- and blemish-free. None of the producers surveyed used economic threshold assessments to determine pesticide levels, though this is a good way to reduce pesticide use, largely because of their unfamiliarity with this method of inte-grated pest management. Farm managers are generally aware of import standards for residue tolerances in the exported products, but most do not have equipment for monitoring residue levels. The studies reveal an overall lack of information and knowledge about risks and safety measures needed for ra-tional pesticide use.

Remarkably high inputs of pesticides are applied in flower plantations, usually inside greenhouses. Rose and carnation producers in Ecuador, for example, generally use an average of

Box 5. (continued)

six fungicides, four insecticides, and three nematicides, along with herbicides. Added to this are nine kinds of fertilizers and soil supplements, often applied daily. These chemicals account for high proportions of total input costs. Studies of Colombia and Costa Rican flower plantations show similar patterns. In Costa Rica, producers of flowers and ornamental plants typically apply extremely toxic nematicides and insecticides, including methyl parathion, metomil, forato, terbufos, and aldicarb, and a variety of fungicides, including benomil, mancozeb, vinclozolin, ferbam, and captan, and several herbicides (diuron, atrazine, and paraquat), as well as growth regulators and hormones. Again, many of these chemicals are applied daily. Since the flowers are *not* subject to FDA pesticide residue standards because they are not edible, producers tend to have little concern about the issue. However, more judicious pesticide use would greatly reduce costs of production and maintain crop yields.

An analysis of pesticide use in Guatemalan snow peas production, drawing on an original assessment done in late 1993 as part of this project, sheds additional light on the problem. This survey of 114 small-scale snow pea producers in the highlands of Guatemala showed that the main common pesticides used in snow peas are thiodan, copper, malation, ziram, diaznon, perfection, and ferbam; the main target pests are "gallina ciega" (*Phyllophaga*), thrips (e.g., *Frankiniella sp.*), white fly (*Homoptera*), Nogero (*Agrotis sp.*), and worms (*Lepidoptera*). The survey also found 51 cases in which farmers used pesticides that are *not* registered by the EPA for use on snow peas; they included brand names Ambush, Mocap, Baytoid, Antrocol, Tamaron, Benlate, Dithane, Agrofos, and Bavistin. In 20 cases, producers used inappropriate pesticides, such as insecticides for diseases or fungicides for insects, because they lacked knowledge about the agrochemicals, sought the cheapest products, or lacked access to other products. Of those surveyed, 95

Box 5. (continued)

percent reported that the costs of pesticides had increased over time. Most producers lived in fear that their produce would be rejected for "low" aesthetic quality. This fear is logical: In 1993, on average, 16 of every 100 pounds of Guatemalan snow pea produced were rejected due to blemishes. Clearly, chemicals are seen as insurance.

Previous surveys of snow pea producers have shown similar patterns of heavy use of a wide variety of pesticides, including products that are not registered by the EPA. For example, Stewart et al (1990), in a survey of 34 snow pea producers found that a significant number were using unregistered pesticides of Dithane (26 percent), Benlate (20.6 percent), Antrocol (38 percent), Aspor (15 percent) and Ambush (9 percent). Another study of 22 snow pea producers found that they used an average of 7 pesticides, including an average of 2 products unregistered by the EPA, and 54 percent of the producers violated the recommended pre-harvest interval.

Sources: Gordon Conroy, ed., *Pesticide Resistance and World Food Production* (London, England: Centre for Environmental Tech-

paste or juice, usually get fewer pesticide applications, since these foods are not subject to strict aesthetic standards. In addition, indigenous NTAE products, such as *quinoa* and *araza*, are produced with much lower chemical inputs, partly because these native crops are less vulnerable to pests, and partly because farmers are familiar with organic farming techniques for such crops. These cases, however, represent only a minute portion of the total NTAE

Box 5. (continued)

nology, 1982). Information based on field data gathered by William Waters, Universidad San Francisco de Quito, Quito, Ecuador, 1993. Castillo et al., 1989, cited in María Trivelato and Catharina Wesseling, "Utilización de plaguicidas en Costa Rica y otros países centroamericanos: aspectos ambientales y de salud ocupacional," in Ana Beatriz Mendizábal P. and Jürgen Weller, eds., *Promesa o Espejismo?* (Panama City, Panama: Programa Regional del Empleo para América Latina y el Caribe, 1992); Richard Fisher, Roberto Caceres, and Danilo Ardon, "Evaluación del Manejo de Plagas y Plaguicidas en Arveja China del Altiplano de Guatemala," unpublished final report, Centro Mesoamericano de Tecnología Apropriada, Instituto de Ciencia y Tecnología Agrícola, and World Resources Institute, Guatemala City, Guatemala, 1994; Polly Hoppin et al., *Pesticide Use in Four Nontraditional Crops in Guatemala: Implications for Residues* (Guatemala City, Guatemala: U.S. Agency for International Development, Regional Office for Central America and Panama, 1994).

production, since most of these crops are very chemical intensive, as previously explained.

Extensive reliance on heavy inputs of synthetic pesticides can jeopardize the sustainability of the NTAE sector. Moreover, these prevailing pesticide use patterns logically influence the economic, environmental, and social impacts of NTAE production, as described in Chapter IV.

IV.
IMPACTS OF NTAE GROWTH: PROMISES AND PROBLEMS

The growth of non-traditional exports has had bittersweet outcomes—both promises and problems. The particular mix of effects depends partly on each country's socio-political context and institutional capacities. On one hand, NTAEs have generated substantial economic benefits and business successes for those involved in the sector. On the other, they entail significant social and ecological costs, inequities, and economic risks—reflecting some common patterns of previous export sectors. These adverse outcomes raise concerns about the sustainability and equity of this strategy and call into question the meaning of NTAEs' "success."

Without attempting to measure *all* the benefits and costs of NTAEs, the following overview will improve understanding of the advantages and disadvantages and the reasons for these results. The outcomes of the NTAE strategy can be assessed in relation to the overall challenge to promote broad-based sustainable development, as depicted earlier in Figure 2. This concept is upheld by many public and private institutions and groups, ranging from international agencies to grassroots activists. Although numerous interpretations are used, there is general agreement that the goals of sustainable agriculture systems are environmental soundness to conserve the natural resource base, social equity to ensure healthy livelihoods for all farmers and workers, and economic productivity over time to provide an adequate quantity and quality of food and fiber to meet present and future requirements.[132] Within this general framework, the fundamental questions related to the NTAE boom are who benefits and how, for what, and for how long.

A. Economic Effects

1. Growth of Export Earnings

The growth rate and value of NTAEs have been impressive. As shown in Figure 9, (and in Figure 2), non-traditional export values from Latin America and the Caribbean, have grown steadily since 1980, reaching approximately $430 million in 1991.[133] Throughout the Caribbean Basin, NTAEs grew at an average annual rate of 15 percent from 1983 to 1991; the value of these exports to the United States reached $100 million in 1991.[134] Growth rates of NTAEs have been very high in individual countries as well. From 1984 to 1989, NTAEs more than doubled in Chile, more than tripled in Costa Rica, and grew by 78 percent in Guatemala.[135] In Ecuador, the value of NTAEs grew 27-fold, from $3 million in 1984 to $75 million in 1994.[136]

Remarkably rapid growth rates are found in several individual crops, such as flowers and specialty vegetables and fruits. In Ecuador and Colombia, flowers are the leading NTAEs.[137] Flower exports from Ecuador increased 15-fold in volume and 30-fold in value between 1985 and 1991.[138] In Central America, Guatemala's snow peas stand out: the total volume exported multiplied seven-fold between 1983 to 1991, from 3.5 million pounds to 24.6 million pounds.[139] This crop represented 80 percent of total snow peas imported into the United States from Mexico and Central America in 1991, compared to 45 percent in 1988.[140] Melons also have remarkably high values and growth rates in Central America. The United States now buys a remarkable share of its total melon imports from Central America; between 1983 and 1993, the share of Central American melons increased from 5 percent to 58 percent of the total imports.[141] In Ecuador, broccoli has only recently surfaced as a significant export crop, but its value rose from zero in 1989 to $552,200 in the first 10 months of 1991.[142] Among the Central American countries, Costa Rica is sometimes regarded as a "star" in NTAE growth. Costa Rica's NTAE value grew 348 percent between 1984 and 1989, led by flowers and ornamental crops.[143]

NTAEs still account for a relatively small proportion of exports from Latin America; nor are they likely to approach the values of such traditional export crops as coffee, cotton, beef, and bananas. Guatemala's NTAEs, for instance, now constitute only 15 percent

Figure 9. Agroexport Growth in Latin America

a. South America

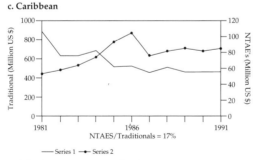
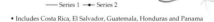

NTAES/Traditionals = 12%

— Series 1 —•— Series 2

b. Central America

NTAES/Traditionals = 8%

— Series 1 —•— Series 2

• Includes Costa Rica, El Salvador, Guatemala, Honduras and Panama

c. Caribbean

NTAES/Traditionals = 17%

— Series 1 —•— Series 2

• Includes Belize, Haiti, Dominican Republic and Jamaica

Source: Roberta Von Haeftan, B. Goodwin and C. Zuvekas. 1993. "LAC Developmental Trends: Background for New Strategy." U.S. Agency for International Development. (Washington, D.C.)

of total value of agricultural exports, and Ecuador's NTAEs still comprise less than 10 percent of total value of agroexport crops.[144] Nevertheless, the net revenues and returns per hectare of NTAEs are remarkably high, usually far exceeding those of traditional crops. Moreover, this sector does represent a growing portion of total export earnings, and many of the products appear to have considerable growth potential.

2. Revenues

The revenues and profitability of NTAEs vary greatly. Export prices and volume exported are important determinants of different net returns on NTAEs. Nevertheless, average returns have been calculated for Central America: in 1989, the average return on NTAE exports (FOB) for the region was $1,476 per hectare.[145] Crops with the highest values per area were, in order: flowers and ornamental plants, fruits, root crops, and vegetables. Nuts and spices were significantly lower, averaging about $500 per hectare.[146] Table 6 shows the values of different products, in terms of gross revenues. In Group I, the highest value products, flowers and ornamental plants rank highest in the proportion of earnings. In Group II, pineapple accounts for half the total value, and melon about a third; in Group III, sesame is the main product, one-third of the total.[147] In South America, flower enterprises have enjoyed particularly high profit margins. A case study of a 100-hectare flower company in Peru, revealed a net profit of $1.4 million in 1992 from carnations alone.[148] This same study estimated that the export earnings of 100 hectares of flowers is equivalent to the earnings of 20,000 hectares of traditional export crops like cotton or sugar cane.

Where producers have switched from locally marketed crops, such as corn and beans, into NTAEs, most enjoy great increases in returns per hectare. In a study of samples of Chilean and Guatemalan smallholders during the late 1980s, for example, gross margins per hectare from NTAEs were more than ten times more than those of basic grain crops produced for the local market.[149] Marginal returns, however, vary considerably, depending on market conditions and farm size. Moreover, average returns for some products have dropped significantly in recent years. For example, snow pea producers in Guatemala have recently experienced very

Table 6. Gross Revenues per Hectare in Central America NTAEs

	Revenues		Revenues
GROUP I >$10,000 (revenue per ha.)			
Cabbage	1.1	Flowers and	
Cucumber	1.2	Plants, etc.	61.2
Papaya	1.5	Chayote	5.2
Strawberry	4.5	Apple	0.5
Percent of NTAEs			**25.5**
Total Revenues ($ million FOB)			**75.2**
GROUP II >$2,000 (revenue per ha.)			
Tomato	1.8	Garlic	0.6
Snow peas	8.2	Cassava	8.0
Carrot	0.7	Pineapple	51.0
Melon	31.9	Celery	0.3
Lettuce	0.5	Potato	1.2
Percent of NTAEs			**35.3**
Total Revenues ($ million FOB)			**104.2**
GROUP III <$2,000 (revenue per ha.)			
Broccoli	4.1	Macadamia	4.2
Brussel sprouts	0.1	African Palm[b]	7.0
Yam	4.6	Sesame	27.5
Pepper	2.2	Mango	0.7
Okra	0.4	Rubber	8.1
Citrus	9.6	Cacao	5.7
Banana	5.8	Peanut	0.4
Watermelon	0.7	Asparagus	0.1
Cauliflower	0.5	Cardamom[a]	0.3
Percent of NTAEs			**27.8**
Total Revenues ($ million FOB)			**82.0**

a. Export date corresponds to 1988.
b. Area date corresponds to 1988.

Source: Andres Achong, "Alcances y limitaciones de las exportaciones agrico-las no tradicionales," in Ana Beatriz Mendizábal P. and Jürgen Weller, eds., *Promesa o Espejismo?* (Panama City, Panama: Programa Regional del Empleo para America Latina y el Caribe, 1992), 398.

low returns and even losses, due mainly to major price declines, high input costs, and import detentions. For other NTAEs, however, revenues continue to be high.

3. Growth of Agribusinesses and investment

As export values have grown, so too has the number of enterprises involved in producing, processing, marketing, and distributing NTAEs. Throughout the region, this includes both foreign and national companies, ranging from fledgling new micro-enterprises to immense transnational firms. The increase in foreign capital has been particularly notable in the NTAE sector, as investors respond to promotion programs and policy incentives.

In Guatemala, though total numbers are difficult to calculate given data limitations, recent estimates suggest that there are around 63,100 NTAE producers in Guatemala, the majority of them smallholders.[150] In addition, there is a growing number of export firms, increasing from 23 in 1980 to approximately 161 in 1992. A recent survey of 22 NTAE export firms showed that their sales grew by 138 percent between 1990 and 1993; over half the firms had increased sales by more than 400 percent.[151] Pinning down exact numbers of NTAE businesses in Guatemala is difficult partly because the sector is highly dynamic; new investors are getting involved, while many producers, especially small poorer farmers, drop out when unable to compete.

In Colombia, over 400 companies have emerged in the flower industry alone, with hundreds of other companies producing high-value fruits and vegetables for export.[152] In Ecuador, NTAEs are in an earlier stage, and the total number of NTAE producers and exporters has been roughly estimated as 1,200.[153] Of these, Ecuador had approximately 70 flower producers in 1991,[154] a relatively small number, since the sector is quite new, but the businesses are fast-growing. Recent changes in export-facilitation laws are likely to induce export firms to expand further in Ecuador, as in other countries.

4. Ancillary Economic Growth Effects and Technical Capacities

The growth of NTAEs has also spawned many ancillary businesses for transport, supplies, packaging, and marketing services.[155]

These enterprises vary from large shipping industries to specialized testing laboratories for pesticide residues to individual intermediary brokers who buy produce from small farmers and sell to exporters. Calculating the total number of these businesses is again difficult since many operate outside formal channels; but there are hundreds in each country adding to the food-commodity chains.

The growth of NTAE producer and export businesses has required and generated the development of new technologies and marketing skills.[156] Successful NTAE enterprises have learned how to effectively manage specialized crops, irrigation, harvesting, and postharvest handling methods. Governments have also tried to help develop such capacities—for instance, by acquiring technical assistance from development agencies or technology transferred from other countries. Developing these capabilities requires considerable time and investment.[157]

The payoffs for building processing capacities and higher quality products can be substantial. The added values of processed products are important benefits in some sectors, even though the initial investments for processing plants can be very high. Often, crops that do not qualify as first-class fresh exports—for example, because of slight cosmetic blemishes or small size—are acceptable and profitable in fruit juices, sauces, canned goods, or processed frozen foods. Chile increased its export income by 8 to 10 percent by processing its surplus products.[158]

Another ostensible benefit of NTAE expansion is its contribution to overall growth of income and gross domestic product (GDP) in Latin American countries. NTAE proponents often presume that export growth causes the economy as a whole to expand: this premise is based largely on economic theory which maintains that export crops mobilize idle resources, exploit "comparative advantage," and produce "linkage effects" in both production and consumption—thereby generating surplus income and increasing growth.[159] In addition, some empirical studies indicate that, in some countries, high GDP growth performance is found along with high rates of export growth in general.[160] However, there is a lack of concrete evidence showing a causal linkage specifically between NTAE growth and broad-based economic growth nationally. Moreover, productivity improvement or some other third factor can explain the increase in both exports and growth. Indeed, the findings have been inconclusive.[161]

Furthermore, though the increase in export values translates into increased foreign exchange earnings, exporting country governments have gained very little indirect revenues or debt alleviation from NTAEs since most governments have eliminated export taxes in recent years to boost export businesses.

5. Economic Uncertainties and Competitive Risks

Although NTAEs clearly have economic benefits, the picture is not all rosy. Prices fluctuate greatly in the NTAE market, as shown in Figure 10, not only over the course of a year, but also from week to week or even day to day. Seasonal changes, shifting consumer preferences, market regulations, and competition and supply from other businesses contribute to the volatility and uncertainty. Although fluctuating prices are characteristic for many agricultural goods, high-value NTAEs are particularly vulnerable to price changes, partly because they are perishable specialty crops. In addition, many of these commodities are trendy luxury items bought by middle-to-high-income consumers with shifting tastes.

Another critical factor that has exacerbated economic risks and reduced the returns of NTAEs is the instability in exchange rates and inflation, both of which are still prevalent in Latin America despite stabilization efforts.[162] The currency valuation in many countries, while more favorable for exporters than in the 1970s and early 1980s, still remains unstable.

Coupled with these uncertainties is the risk of market saturation. Although some market studies suggest that demand for NTAEs will continue to rise, predictions do not always translate into reality.[163] Market growth may decline or may not be sufficient to absorb increasing supplies. Significant price declines have already occurred for some products—farmers who grow snow peas, for instance, have incurred major losses partly because of market saturation. Competition exacerbates these risks and difficulties. As noted by Barham et al. (1992), "After all, how many mangos or macadamia nuts can North Americans be expected to eat, even at lower prices?"[164]

Figure 10. Examples of Price Fluctuations of NTAEs
(Using Wholesale Prices, USDA, 1990)

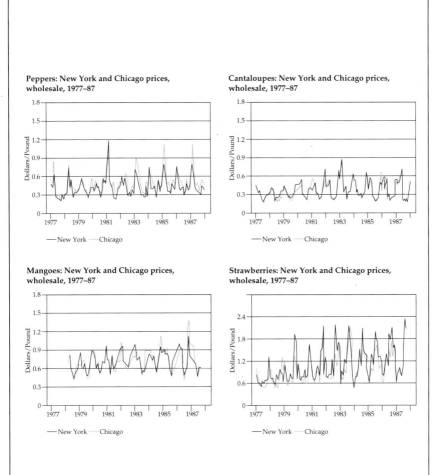

Source: Richard Brown, Richard, and Nydia Suarez. 1991. *U.S. Markets for Caribbean Basin Fruits and Vegetables: Selected Characteristics for 17 Fresh and Frozen Imports.* U.S. Department of Agriculture. Economic Research Service. Washington, D.C.

Poorer NTAE producers and businesses are more vulnerable to economic risks and suffer greater proportional losses compared to more capitalized businesses. Generally, small producers also lack access to credit, technical services, and market information, compounding their difficulties in planning ahead and responding to changes in market demands. Most poorer farmers have little or no chance to negotiate for better prices, partly because they have less bargaining power vis-a-vis powerful foreign buyers. A sudden price decline in the United States decreases prices at every level of the market, usually creating the heaviest burden for producers, especially for poorer farmers. Recently, in Guatemala, for example, when market prices for snow peas were extremely low, it was not worthwhile for smallholders to transport their produce to market. Much of the crop rotted, forcing many people into dire misfortune.

The NTAE business is highly competitive—not only among national producers within a country, but also among countries of the region and African and Asian nations that are starting to grow the same crops. Everyone vies for relatively narrow niche markets. In many of the markets, competition also exists with producers in importing countries. The NTAE promotion programs and policies supported by USAID also help create this competitive climate. Although competition can help stimulate investments, it also heightens pressure in agroexport business and can contribute to inequitable distributional impacts. In other words, large capitalized producers survive, while poorer ones are often squeezed out.

B. Socioeconomic Issues: Distributional Impacts and Nutrition Questions

Based on economic indicators, the NTAE boom has been called a success by some analysts.[165] But other dimensions must be considered. Who are the main beneficiaries of the NTAE boom? Is NTAE growth helping to alleviate hunger and rural poverty? Evidence shows NTAE growth has mixed impacts on the distribution of benefits in Latin America, ranging from exclusionary growth concentrated in the hands of a few companies, to relatively broad-based involvement of poor rural farmers in a few cases.

1. Concentration of Benefits in NTAEs

In most Latin American countries, the main beneficiaries of NTAE growth are large companies, including both transnational corporations (TNCs) and large national and foreign investors. These businesses profit most from NTAEs, largely because they can afford to make the very high capital outlays necessary to compete in this market and meet the costs of complying with strict market demands. Many of these enterprises have also benefitted from NTAE-promotion programs.

The inequitable concentration of land and benefits in the NTAE sector has been verified in a number of countries. In Chile, for example, "while the macroeconomy has benefitted by the expansion of the fruit sector, these benefits have not been widely distributed throughout the society..."[166] Three of the top four firms in Chile's NTAE production are owned by transnational corporations.[167] In Central America, transnationals account for approximately 25 percent of the total NTAE production, and they also handle distribution and transport for a large percent of the exports.[168] This hold is strongest in fruits and vegetables. For instance, Del Monte in Costa Rica and Dole in Honduras market almost all pineapple exports.[169] Both firms directly produce most of their pineapple exports and contract the rest to medium and large national growers. Del Monte and Chiquita control about a third of the 12,000 hectares of melons in Central America.[170] Chiquita (United Brands) first invested in the melon business in 1975, under the name of PATSA, which bought melons from some 90 growers and also planted at least 600 hectares. In Costa Rica, using the name Agroexpo, Chiquita buys melons from 46 producers and cultivates about 340 hectares. Del Monte cultivates some 600 hectares of melons in Costa Rica and exports the bulk of mangos and papaya from Costa Rica.[171] In addition, the transnational corporations produce and market citrus, strawberries, and other products. Coca Cola has become one of the main producers of citrus and orange juice in Belize and Brazil.[172]

The strength of the transnational corporations rests largely on their economic power and competitive advantages and on their long-established business in the region. Chiquita (United Brands/ Fruit), Dole (Standard Fruit Company) and Del Monte created strong market networks in bananas and good access to information and technology which allowed them to rapidly expand into newer export products.[173] Their economic status also enables them to shift production from one site to another when profitable and to gain privileges such as tax exemptions from governments in export policies. Another leading category of NTAE beneficiaries known as *empresarios* includes both large national companies and foreign entrepreneurs, mainly from the United States. These companies generally have substantial capital, even though some of the farms are mid-sized. They have also been among the principal beneficiaries of USAID's promotion programs. In Central America, such firms account for an estimated 40 percent of NTAEs, mainly flowers, melons, ornamental plants, vegetables, oils, and nuts.[174] At least 1500 of these companies operate in Central America, but fewer than 100 dominate production.[175] The concentration of large businesses in Costa Rica and Honduras NTAEs are shown in Table 7.[176] In Ecuador as well, mainly *empresarios* benefit from NTAEs, accounting for most production and marketing. Many are bankers and industrialists that use NTAE investments to diversify their portfolios. In Colombia, the patterns in NTAE distribution are similar to those in other countries; but the flower business is even more well-developed and capitalized.

Foreign investors play a prominent role in large and medium-size operations throughout the region. According to one study, approximately two thirds of the flower plantations in Ecuador involve foreign investments, mainly from Colombia, Holland, and the United States.[177] In Costa Rica, foreign investors dominate production of flowers, ornamental plants, citrus, and macadamia nuts. Of the 14 largest flower growers, only two are actually Costa Rican and one U.S. company, American Flowers, produces half of the country's flower exports. Costa Rica's macadamia lands are 40 percent foreign owned; and Matas de Costa Rica, which occupies 1,320 hectares, and accounts for one third of the nation's ornamental plant exports, belongs to a U.S. import company.[178]

In Paraguay, where soybeans are the main NTAE grown, production has become increasingly dominated by large mechanized farms owned mainly by national and foreign investors.[179] Changes in land ownership over time have favored wealthier farmers. Moreover, farms absorb less labor as size increases. Economic

Table 7. Concentration of Largest NTAE Businesses in Costa Rica and Honduras (in percentage)

	Costa Rica (1986)			Honduras (1988)		
		Single			Single	
	No. of Businesses	Largest Business (%)	Three Largest (%)	No. of Businesses	Largest Business (%)	Three Largest (%)
Flowers	79	31.1	53.6	2	n.d.	n.d.
Foliage	41	23.9	45.3	4	48.5	n.d.
Ornamental Plants	92	20.0	35.6	15	20.9	53.3
Vegetables[1]	28	51.3	69.7	17	39.7	77.8
Roots[2]	33	16.8	33.0	8	24.3	n.d.
Pineapple	22	94.9	97.3	10	96.3	98.3
Strawberry[3]	13	26.2	62.7	25	52.7	72.3
Bananas	31	32.1	59.7	25	22.3	47.2
Other Fruits[4]	7	94.0	98.7	20	62.8	84.4
Cacao	6	63.2	95.6	8	34.9	79.1
Seeds and Fruit	n.d.	n.d.	n.d.	6	81.6	92.7
Oils, Pepper	n.d.	n.d.	n.d.	6	40.3	78.1

Notes:
1. In Costa Rica: chayote; in Honduras: legumes
2. In Costa Rica: yuca; in Honduras: roots and tubers
3. In Costa Rica: strawberry; in Honduras: citrus
4. In Costa Rica: papaya; in Honduras: "The remaining fresh fruits of tropical origin" (i.e. principally melon)
n.d. = no data available

Sources: Jürgen Weller, "Las exportaciones agricolas notradicionales y sus efectos en el empleo y los ingresos," in Ana Beatriz Mendizábal P. and Jürgen Weller, eds., *Promesa o Espejismo?* (Panama City, Panama: Programa Regional del Empleo para America Latina y el Caribe, 1992), 155.

crises in Paraguay have exacerbated these disparities. Chile's fruit export boom also helped concentrate production and polarize the agrarian structure between large and small farmers.[180]
Another related trend found in some NTAE sectors is the growing concentration of land. As several studies have documented, in some countries, large businesses have accumulated land in agroexport crops while poorer farmers have been squeezed out of this market and pushed onto marginal land.[181] NTAEs tend to elevate land rents and values, thereby pushing out smallholders who can no longer compete. In Chile, for example, during the 1980s, large-scale fruit producers bought out small *parceleros* who lacked the capital, information, and credit needed to invest in export fruit crops.[182] These kinds of trends have also occurred in Costa Rica and Paraguay and even in Guatemala in recent years. For example, according to a recent study, a sample of medium to large producers (30 to 200 hectares) in the Guatemalan highlands "has been accumulating land at a rapid rate," while very poor smallholders confront increasing constraints. Clearly, this shows that more capitalized producers have gained a competitive advantage over time.[183]
The question of scale is complicated for many NTAE crops, especially flowers and specialty vegetables, because the average farm size is generally quite small, compared with that of farms for traditional exports; this does *not* mean however, that they have low economic status. The average size of Ecuador's flower plantations, for instance, is under 10 hectares. Yet, these producers clearly are not typical "small-scale" poor farmers but are highly capitalized businesses. Thus, farm size *per se* is not an adequate indication of the prosperity of any NTAE enterprise. Indeed, capital endowment is usually more important in interpreting "scale."

2. Critical Constraints for Poor Smallholders

Evidence from several countries shows that resource-poor farmers usually encounter major difficulties entering and competing in the NTAE market.[184] In nearly all countries, these farmers tend to lack access to the credit, capital, technical services, and information needed to succeed in the agroexport business. Usually, smallholders are unfamiliar with the export crops and production technology; most tend to lack entrepreneurial skills and experience with institutions such as export firms. Training courses and technical services rarely reach them.

Gaining entry to the market is particularly difficult for poor farmers in countries, such as Chile, Ecuador, and Paraguay, where NTAE programs have paid little attention to them. In Chile, "small farmers have not been major participants in the expansion [of the fruit sector] largely because government policies with respect to credit, technical assistance, and research restricted rather than enhanced their access to fruit production."[185] Even if they do get involved in NTAE production, poorer farmers often get squeezed out, as noted previously.

In Ecuador, resource-poor farmers rarely gain access to technical assistance from PROEXANT for NTAEs. A basic obstacle is the fee required for the services; joining the Federation of Exporters costs at least $100 initially and $25 per month thereafter.[186] Although this fee is minor for wealthy companies, it can be prohibitive for a new entrepreneur with minimal capital. Managers of Ecuador's NTAE promotion programs and banks interviewed in 1993 stated that they explicitly discouraged small poorer farmers from embarking on NTAE business, mainly because it seems too risky to them.[187] If the present trends continue in Ecuador, poor producers will remain largely excluded.

These trends of concentration and social disparities in the NTAE sector are partly tied to inequitable socioeconomic structures in Latin American agriculture, yet, they are also partly attributable to predominant NTAE policies which underemphasize the social impacts of production.

3. Involvement of Smallholders' Associations

Some small-scale poor producers in Latin America have benefitted directly from NTAE production, especially when they are organized into cooperatives and other associations. This has occurred in Guatemala, El Salvador, Bolivia, and Costa Rica. Guatemala provides a good, albeit unique, illustration of poor smallholders' substantial involvement in NTAEs. According to PROEXAG estimates, some 8,000 Guatemalan smallholders (those with relatively small land and capital endowments) grow snow peas for export,[188] though other estimates suggest as many as

10,000.[189] Approximately 90 percent of snow peas in the country are grown by these smallholders, mostly in the highlands near Guatemala City.[190] At least 4,000 others produce a large percentage of vegetables such as broccoli and cauliflower.[191] These small-scale farmers were able to enter into this market because their labor costs were relatively low, they had access to and previous experience in vegetable markets, they were organized to a fair degree, and to some extent, they received support from development projects.

In general, cooperatives can help provide such support. By the end of 1989, there were 524 agricultural cooperatives in Guatemala, each having an average of 111 members;[192] but only a few of these cooperatives have been successful in NTAE production. The most renowned cooperative in Guatemala is Cuatro Pinos. *(See Box 6.)* Supported by donors including USAID, this 1,700-member co-op developed an effective enterprise for producing and marketing vegetables, mainly snow peas.[193] In the 1980s, it thrived, and members' incomes increased. However, in the 1990s, like other co-ops and small farmers generally, it has run up against considerable economic difficulties, due mainly to falling prices and pesticide residue violations. Consequently, many members have dropped out of this market. Nevertheless, Cuatro Pinos represents a unique experience for smallholders.

In Bolivia, small-scale poor farmers are also involved in the production of NTAEs, often through cooperatives and traditional organizations. The traditional communal customs and labor systems of Bolivia's indigenous communities sometimes serve as a basis for managing NTAE marketing. Many smallholders produce and market *quinoa*, a traditional protein-rich grain that indigenous peoples have cultivated for centuries using little or no chemical inputs. In recent years, this grain has been rediscovered by devotees of natural food in North America and Europe, opening a niche market and export opportunities for Andean smallholders. *(See Box 7.)* Other smallholder cooperatives that use organic production methods have been established for coffee and chocolate as well. *(See Chapter V.)*

Difficulties notwithstanding, these cases illustrate that the benefits of high-value export products do sometimes reach poor farmers and could possibly be spread more broadly, if appropriate socioeconomic and political conditions were in place. Experi-

Box 6. The Cuatro Pinos Cooperative in Guatemala

The Cuatro Pinos Cooperative, located in the Department of Sacatapequez in the highlands near Guatemala City, is often cited as a unique and successful case of how smallholders can benefit from NTAEs. Started after the 1976 earthquake with the assistance of Swiss government aid, the co-op was initially engaged in community development, reconstruction, literacy, training, and production of domestic food crops. In 1980, Cuatro Pinos began growing non-traditional export vegetables—mainly snow peas, pod beans, broccoli, cauliflower, and brussels sprouts—under a contract with ALCOSA, a subsidiary of Hanover Brands. In 1981, the co-op began exporting vegetables directly to United States markets and built its own processing and freezing plant, with assistance from USAID; in the next few years, it expanded into the European market.

The co-op is unusually large, with approximately 1,700 members in the early 1990s, more than an eight-fold increase since 1979. Most of the families are indigenous peoples who are quite poor and have small-scale farms, ranging from a few hundred square feet to three hectares per household. The co-op covers a total population of 12,000 and the average household size is 6.7 people.

Cuatro Pinos has been successful in the NTAE business in several ways; it has produced and exported large volumes of high-value vegetable products, benefitted numerous rural families, and developed sophisticated managerial and technical capacities. The experience has also encouraged the establishment of other Guatemalan enterprises and cooperatives that market a diversity of vegetables.

A comprehensive analysis of Cuatro Pinos showed positive income effects for the producer families involved during the 1980s. It also showed overall improvements in the members' quality of life, in terms of basic needs and housing conditions. NTAEs also facilitated the involvement of women in the labor force for processing and production. However, an updated

---

Box 6. (continued)

analysis in 1992 by the same researchers showed that between 1988 and 1992, the co-op and its members experienced a fall in real incomes, largely due to fluctuations in prices, technical inefficiency of production and marketing, increasingly strict import regulations—particularly pesticide residue standards—and, sometimes, difficulties gaining access to land. As a result, many farmers decreased or even ceased NTAE production. Now, most of these smallholder co-op members cultivate a wider mixture of export crops, locally marketed crops, along with corn and beans for their own household food needs, thus spreading risks.

These difficulties illustrate a pattern found elsewhere—that the medium- and longer-term effects of NTAEs are tenuous for small farmers. Strong organizational capacities can help overcome some constraints, but smallholders will continue facing serious challenges, especially if policies and services do not support their involvement.

What effect the War.

Sources: Joaquim von Braun, D. Hotchkiss, and M. Immink. 1989. *Nontraditional Export Crops in Guatemala: Effects on Production, Income and Nutrition.* Research Report # 73. Washington, D.C. International Food Policy Research Institute; and Immink, Maarten et al. 1993. "Nontraditional Export Crops Among Smallholder Farmers and Production, Income, Nutrition, and Quality of Life Effects." Washington D.C.: IFPRI.

---

ence shows that farmer organizations such as co-ops provide many benefits and are virtually essential, though not sufficient, if small farmers are to survive in the NTAE business.[194] These and other associations help reduce risks, increase access to information and services, and improve the bargaining power of poorer producers.

Box 7. *Quinoa* Production in Bolivia

In the Southern Altiplano region of Potosí in Bolivia, thousands of small-scale indigenous farmers produce *quinoa* for export through cooperatives. An illustrative example is the Central de Cooperación Agricola: Operación Tierra, which has about 250 to 300 members. This cooperative sells about 80 tons of *quinoa* per year, 60 to 70 percent for export to Europe and the United States. The co-op's annual export earnings from this crop total about $70,000. Members plant a unique indigenous variety, called *quinoa real*, which is in higher demand than other varieties and is cultivated largely on communal lands, using traditional communal forms of labor organization. Most of the labor is manual, except for land preparation, which is done largely by tractors owned by the cooperative. The product is sold directly to specialty food distributors and socially conscious health food stores; so benefits are channeled directly to the community. Outside this co-op, at least 4,000 other Bolivian smallholders are producing *quinoa* for export in an association called *Anapqui*, which generates between $300,000 and $400,000 yearly. Unlike Operación Tierra, this large group markets its product through the transnational company Nestlé; even so, smallholders have made considerable gains by participating in the global supermarket.

Source: Kevin Healy, Interamerican Foundation, personal communication, 1994.

---

4. Additional Challenges for Smallholders
    In most countries no organizations for poor farmers exist or, if they do, generally lack sufficient technical, managerial, and financial resources to produce and market NTAEs efficiently. Even where there are farmer organizations, as in Guatemala, co-ops face such market constraints as low prices and poor transport systems.

Furthermore, the development of NTAE cooperatives depends largely on external support, both for funds and technical assistance. Cuatro Pinos, for example, has been financed generously by the Swiss Development Agency, USAID, and other donors. NTAE associations in Bolivia have received financing and technical support from the Swedish Corporation for Technical Assistance, the German Government, and the Interamerican Foundation. For example, the Interamerican Foundation provided $380,000 spread out over 16 years, to one NTAE cooperative alone (El Ceibo) to assist in land purchases, administration, training, and other operational activities.[195] Without this external funding, co-ops probably would not have been effective in NTAEs, especially given the usual lack of government support.

A few cases indicate that external support, though essential to start up an organization, can be phased down or out over time, after a co-op has established an economically viable business and good management skills. However, lack of financial resources for smallholders continue to thwart the sustainability and equity of NTAEs.[196] In addition, poorer producers, even if organized, face impediments or biases in access to credit and fair prices for their produce.[197]

Another way for poorer farmers to get involved in NTAE production is through contract farming. In contracting arrangements, an exporter usually provides working capital or credit, technical assistance, and post-harvest handling facilities to smallholders who cannot gain access to these services independently. In return, smallholders usually agree to provide labor and land and commit their harvests (or a fixed share) to the contracting firm under specified terms. Generally, the contracting firms establish strict conditions for delivery dates, product quality and grading, and credit-reimbursement schedules.

In some countries, contract farming with small NTAE farmers has been fairly common. In Guatemala, for example, a 1993 survey found that 11 out of 13 vegetable-processing firms used contract farming to get crops for processing and export.[198] Some agribusiness firms prefer such contracting with smallholders because these companies can usually get better terms and higher profits (due partly to small farmers' undervaluation of their labor costs) and because smallholders are often considered the most efficient producers. Contract farming can also benefit the smallholders in some circumstances, but experience shows that contractual arrangements often entail greater risks and disadvantages for smallholders, who are often vulnerable to unfair pricing and have weak bargaining power vis-a-vis buyers. Sometimes buyers consider contracting with smallholders too risky, as in Ecuador where NTAE exporters fear a lack of quality control.[199] In Chile as well, agroexport firms are reluctant to contract with smallholders. There, the high transaction costs involved in working with multiple producers is seen as the main constraint.[200]

Such complications in contract farming add to the diverse impediments for poor producers in the NTAE sector. These difficulties were summarized in a 1993 public presentation by representatives of an association of Guatemalan farmers who produce vegetables for export. (See Box 8.) Although these farmers had benefitted in the mid-1980s from rapid NTAE growth, they noted experiencing increasingly serious economic risks and technical obstacles over time. They also stressed that the intense competitiveness in NTAEs has undermined traditional social cohesion among farmers and community members, as market obligations create individualistic behavior.[201] In addition, parents often remove their children from school to work in NTAE fields, thwarting their educational development.

5. Distribution of Revenues in the Market Chain

Another important issue in considering the impact of NTAEs is the distribution of economic benefits and price margins at different levels in the market chain. As in other agricultural sectors, prices and values increase at every stage—from producers, to brokers, importers-exporters, distributors, and retailers. Specific profit figures at each level would help reveal these gaps, but such data is often confidential and difficult to acquire. Estimated price breakdowns of various fruits and vegetables, based largely on data from the USDA and field studies, show the prices at different levels when imported into the United States. (See Figure 11.) For example, in 1994, U.S. shoppers spent an average of $3.99 per pound for snow peas, and producers in Guatemala received about 18 cents

Box 8. Guatemalan Smallholders Highlight Constraints in
NTAE Vegetable Production

Recent participatory workshops involving NTAE smallholders revealed local peoples' concerns about conditions in
this sector. In the Guatemalan highlands, where thousands of
indigenous farmers are involved in NTAEs, all members of the
households—women, men, children, and elders—work together to produce and market snow peas and other vegetables
for export. Household members from the village of Sacatapequez explained that many of these NTAE-producing families
experienced significant changes in their lives when they
started selling snow peas in the 1980s. When prices were favorable, most increased their incomes and as a result they often
improved their housing conditions and purchased clothing or
other basic items.

However, in the 1990s, as international prices dropped and
pest problems became worse and soils became exhausted,
these families have suffered serious economic difficulties and
failures. "The instability of prices, along with the rising costs of
agrochemical inputs, and the increasing numbers of producers,
and the tired land" have frustrated many families. Meanwhile,
many intermediary brokers offer unfair prices for the product.
As one Sacatapequez producer stated, "the powerful actors
playing with prices that they want...are killing us little by little." Discussions among the small producers revealed that
women have even less bargaining power than men in negotiat-
ing prices.

The family's labor is vital to the production process. Yet, it
is undervalued, not only in formal statistics but also by the
people themselves. When asked to describe the costs required
for NTAE production, smallholder farmers consistently do not
account for their own time and labor. This is particularly true
for women, even though work in NTAE fields compounds
their overall labor load. Moreover, parents often remove their
children from schools at an early age to put them to work on

Box 8. (continued)

NTAEs. Farmers also complained that they have been forced into using increasing amounts of expensive agrochemicals, yet they lack information and protection for the application of pesticides.

At an intersectoral workshop on the sustainability of non-traditional export production, held in Antigua, Guatemala in late 1993, representatives of a farmers' association articulated the principal concerns they had about NTAE production. They referred to their experience in the area of Patzun, Chimaltenango, but their conclusions are more widely relevant:

"We affirm that only 5 percent of the population has benefited from the production of non-traditional agroexports, and 95 percent of the population has become poorer. Our living conditions are inferior to those that we had before starting NTAE production. We refer to some salient points from our experience:

- When we started NTAE production in 1980, we received Q13.00 per *quintal* of broccoli (one *quintal* = 100 lbs), when the exchange rate was one *quetzal* = one dollar. Now, we receive 50.00 *quetzals*, approximately $8.63.
- We have increased dependence on fertilizers, insecticides and other inputs, but the quality of these inputs has decreased. For example, when before we used 15 pounds of fertilizer per *cuerda* (one *cuerda* = 0.04 hectare approx.), now we need one and a half *quintales*.
- The costs of agricultural inputs, land rents, labor and transport have increased considerably, while interest rates for credit have increased.
- When we sell our product, buyers do not pay cash, and they impose a minimum 10 percent discount, and this amount increases if the product is not the desired quality. But if we complain about the discount, the company threatens not to buy our product.
- Intermediaries and transport companies have become rich in NTAE systems, while producers have become poorer.

Box 8. (continued)

- We suffer from health problems that we never had before…due to exposure to agrochemical poisons and the difficult work.
- Our family life has been harmed by this work in NTAEs. Little time is available to spend on child raising.
- There is no time for community life.… We are so preoccupied with taking care of the [vegetable] products; We do not have time to meet and interact with our neighbors, and we have become individualistic, without interest in others.
- We have lost respect for Mother Earth. We now perceive it as an instrument [for producing high yields of export crops].
- We receive poor treatment from buyers and exporter companies. We are losing our liberty and independence, and if there is a problem in production, they blame it on us.
- Many of us have lost the little that we had."

Although many smallholders in the 1990s share similar negative perspectives and have therefore given up on producing vegetables for export, others continue to produce diverse high-value export crops along with subsistence crops on their modest plots. While they recognize the clear risks involved, some farming families still gamble on growing a small amount of export crops.

Source: Marcelo Mucia, 1993. "Sostenibilidad Social: la experiencia de los productores de Patzun, Chimaltenango," en *Sostenibilidad de la Producción Agrícola Notradicional de Exportacion por Pequeños Productores en Guatemala;* Memorias del taller, Guatemala: Instituto de Nutrición de Centroamerica y Panama and World Resources Institute. (Translated by L.A. Thrupp); Victor Puac, 1993, "Informe de la Evaluación Preliminar sobre Impactos de Cultivos Notradicionales en las Condiciones de la Mujer." Unpublished paper. Guatemala/Washington D.C.: World Resources Institute.

Figure 11. Price Levels In the Market Chain, May 1994

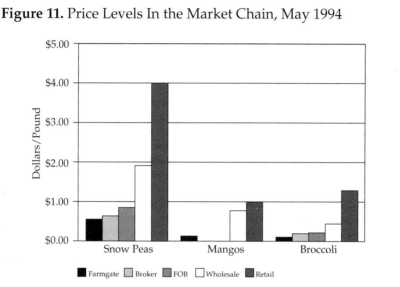

Source: Prices for snow peas and broccoli are from Guatemala; farmgate, broker and FOB prices are from PROEXAG, 5/94, unpublished data; and for wholesale prices are *USDA/Market News* 5/94; Retail (in Washington, D.C.) Safeway, 5/94. Mangos are from Ecuador: farmgate PROEXANT, 5/94; wholesale prices are *USDA/Market News* 5/94; Retail (in Washington, D.C.) Safeway, 5/94.

per pound; For mangos, the U.S. consumer spent 99 cents per pound, and the producer received about 8 cents.[202] Other evidence reveals that small producers of high-value agroexports tend to receive a small percentage of the amount earned from the final sale.[203] A previous analysis of revenues in the NTAE market chain in Costa Rica and Honduras also reveals the distribution at different stages, as illustrated in Table 8. In general, poorer producers receive lower prices and profit margins than medium and large producers do, partly because of unequal exchange relations and a lack of bargaining power in market transactions.[204]

Table 8. NTAE Revenue Distribution in Different Stages, (in price percent CIP/Miami) in Costa Rica

	Melon	Coffee	Pineapple	Bananas	Cocoa
Agriculture	4.6	3.8	9	22.5	6.6
Manual labor	6.6	14.6	3.8	9.0	22.5
Other production costs	14.1	19.6	13.5	11.3	27.4
Producer earnings	8.6	13.7	15.4	6.6	37.5
Packing	14.6	14.2	15.6	11.3	8.2
National Transport.	2.6	0.9	2.3	1.7	1.3
Port	0.5	0.7	0.6	0.4	0.8
Export earnings	24.4	28.4	9.2	31.6	-5.6
International transport.	28.6	8.0	39.6	28.3	7.9
*CIF/Miami	100.0	100.0	100.0	100.0	100.0
Subsidies	20.1	4.6	16.8	19.3	23.8

Source: Jürgen Weller, "Las exportaciones agricolas no tradicionales y sus efectos en el empleo y los ingresos," in Ana Beatriz Mendizábal P. and Jürgen Weller, eds., *Promesa o Espejismo?* (Panama City, Panama: Programa Regional del Empleo para America Latina y el Caribe, 1992), 153.

* Figures are rounded

Although these patterns are similar for many other commercialized crops, the price gaps in the NTAE market chain are particularly wide.[205] Reducing the number of intermediaries in the NTAE commodity chain generally raises values and improves the profit margins for producers who remain in the market.

6. Food Security and Nutritional Impacts

Do NTAEs help improve livelihoods by alleviating hunger among rural poor people? Answering this question is not easy, partly because NTAE growth is relatively new and its impacts are varied, and partly because detailed local-level data on nutrition levels and food availability is lacking. However, survey evidence from Guatemala on vegetable producers in the highland region shows varied effects. In the Cuatro Pinos study, "at same income levels, export-producing farm households spend less of their additional income on food than traditional-crop households.... Additional income increases calorie acquisition significantly, but at decreasing rates at the margin..."[206] In many cases, the nutritional status of NTAE producers remained the same or deteriorated (compared to non-NTAE households), but not significantly. Overall, in Cuatro Pinos, household income was found to be the significant determinant of nutritional status among both women and children.

Another study of five highland communities in Solola and Chimaltenango also showed that income increases from NTAEs did *not* always translate into improved nutritional status.[207] In fact, among the lowest-income quartile of the sample, NTAE families consumed *fewer* calories and proteins than those that were not producing NTAEs. This occurred mainly because men tend to control expenditures from increased income, usually using the money for agricultural inputs, paying debts, and sometimes purchasing more land.[208] When women earn their own wages *and* control the expenditures, however, they generally spend income on food for their family. These findings show that gender relations make a significant difference in the overall impact of NTAE growth on well-being. Most women prefer to maintain independent economic activities and to grow subsistence crops so they can meet family food needs.[209] Another recent study in the Guatemalan Oriente region reported similar findings.[210]

Other studies show that the change from consumption of locally produced staples (grown on a farmer's own land) to purchasing such foods from cash-crop earnings in general can lower the quality of diet as purchased foods tend to be less nutritious; for instance, one comprehensive analysis argues that pre-school children are subjected to "substantial nutrition stress" in households involved in the rapid commercialization of agriculture, unlike those in subsistence-based households.[211] Furthermore, recent price declines affecting vegetables exported from Central America have decreased income for small vegetable producers—which can lower their nutritional status.[212]

As a more general concern, many analysts and farmers have pointed out that investments in export growth and the associated land-use change reduce investments in crops for local markets, and converts small farmers into rural workers; these trends have led to declines in health and nutrition status—thus jeopardizing local food security.[213] Similarly, analysts have noted that the focus by development agencies and governments on export-oriented development policies diverts attention from domestic food needs. The growth rate for export crops in Latin America was twice that for subsistence crops for the period 1964–84, according to the United Nations, and between 1981 and 1988, *per capita* production of grains fell 7 percent; moreover, evidence in many Latin American countries shows that the poor have grown poorer and often cannot afford to buy foods which are being imported in growing volumes in most Latin American countries; and the rural poor's declining access to productive land has also exacerbated the general fall in living standards.[214] In many areas, the nutritional status of children has worsened over the past decade. The debt crisis along with reduction in public investment in rural development aggravated the lack of attention to local food needs. Such trends show that the needs of the rural poor are not yet being adequately met through the present patterns of outward-oriented development, especially given the accompanying neglect of national food needs. Often, income benefits of exports do not "trickle down" as anticipated. [215] More research is needed to determine the specific effects of NTAE production on the availability and consumption of food among the poor.

C. Employment Impacts of Non-traditional Agroexports

1. Growing Numbers of Jobs
NTAE growth generates employment in all stages. Although the specific labor requirements vary for different products, Table 9 shows that the leading NTAE crops like flowers, vegetables, and fruits, entail much more labor per hectare on average than traditional crops.[216] This labor intensity is welcome in most rural areas of Latin America, where jobs are needed. In Guatemala, snow peas production is particularly labor-intensive, requiring an average of

663 labor days per hectare—about 11 times more than corn or beans (58 and 61 labor days, respectively).[217] In Ecuador and Colombia, flower production involves an average of 200 person-days per hectare,[218] compared to 150 person days per hectare for potato production, 44 for coffee, and 33 for bananas.[219] Labor intensity varies according to farm size and technology, among other factors. Large farms tend to produce any given crop with less labor per hectare than small farms.[220]

Estimates of total NTAE-related jobs are usually rough, given survey limitations and the dynamic nature of the labor force. In Colombia, the flower industry employs an estimated 80,000 workers and accounts for some 50,000 jobs in ancillary industries, such as packaging and transport.[221] Total estimated wages are $65 million per year.[222] In Guatemala, estimates from the Bank of Guatemala and two field studies showed approximately 14,000 jobs in NTAE processing firms and about 21,000 full-time jobs in production, with jobs in ancillary industries estimated at about 5,000, for a total of around 40,000 full-time jobs.[223] This total represents a ten-fold increase from 1978. In Guatemala, as elsewhere, a significant proportion of NTAE jobs are seasonal or temporary, which partly accounts for the difficulty in obtaining exact counts. In Central American countries, total full-time jobs in NTAEs reached an estimated 12,400 in Costa Rica and 11,890 in Honduras by 1991.[224] *(See Table 10.)* In Costa Rica, 39 percent of the total NTAE labor is in flowers and ornamental plants; in Honduras 52 percent of total labor is in fruits. The effect of NTAEs on the rural labor market in these countries has been small so far (5 percent and 2 percent of total agricultural labor, respectively); but in some concentrated areas, such as pineapple plantations in Costa Rica, job generation has been great and has induced a large wave of seasonal migration.[225] Indirect employment generation in marketing, transport and agrochemical supplies is estimated at 2,400 in Costa Rica and 850 in Honduras.[226] In Ecuador, estimates of numbers of jobs in the NTAE sector cover a broad range, from 31,000 to 53,000 people;[227] but these figures do not specify how many jobs are permanent and how many temporary.

Many NTAE jobs involve learning new skills, especially in processing. Some of these skills—related to quality control, classification, and preparations for freezing, canning or juicing—are highly

Table 9. Comparative Labor Requirements

Crop	Labor Required	Seasonality
Guatemala		
Corn	58 md/ha	
Beans	61 md/ha	
Broccoli	197 md/ha	
Cauliflower	276 md/ha	
Snowpeas	663 md/ha	
Melons	172 md/ha	
Okra	488 md/ha	
Carnations	340 md/ha	
Mexico		
Cauliflower	21.4 md/ha	89% in 3 months
Broccoli	27.2 md/ha	92% in 3 months
Tomatoes	91.3 md/ha	51% in 3 months
Asparagus	324.0 md/ha	69% in 3 months
Strawberries	300.4 md/ha	51% in 3 months
Chile		
Fruit	150–200 md/ha	2/3 temporary work

specialized for particular products. In some cases, as in Guatemala, this kind of specialization can bring workers a daily wage 5 to 10 percent more than other workers' wages.[228]

2. Female Labor As a Notable Feature of NTAEs
    Throughout Latin America and the Caribbean, a large proportion of those working in both production and processing are women. This significant and widespread trend in the rural wage

Table 9. (continued)

Crop	Labor Required	Seasonality
Central America		
Strawberries	150 md/ha	high seasonality
Pineapples	100 md/ha	many permanent jobs
Melon	100 md/ha	high seasonality
Yuca-Papaya	50 md/ha	labor at harvest
Mangos	<50 md/ha	mostly permanent
Honduras		
Melon	210 md/ha	highly seasonal
Shrimp	109 md/ha	4-month cycle only
(artisanal)		
Asparagus	133 md/ha	mostly permanent
Cucumbers	105 md/ha	50–50 seasonal
Honeydew	28 md/ha	most at harvest

Source: Cited in Michael Carter, B. Barham, D. Mesbah, and D. Stanley, "Agroexports and the Rural Resource Poor in Latin America: Policy Options for Achieving Broadly-Based Growth," draft paper, University of Wisconsin, Land Tenure Center, Madison, Wisconsin, 1993; and James Fox, Kenneth Swanberg, and Thomas Mehen, "Agribusiness Assessment: Guatemala Case Study, draft paper, U.S. Agency for International Development, Washington, D.C. 1994.

labor force has accompanied the globalization of non-traditional food systems. Of course, traditionally, women have participated actively in farming throughout the region, but until recently, they usually worked as unpaid and uncounted workers in subsistence farming. The NTAE industry increasingly engages women in wage-based rural labor. *(See Box 9.)*

In Colombia, for example, 80 percent of the 80,000 workers in the flower industry are women.[229] In Ecuador, about 69 percent of

87

Table 10. Employment in Non-traditional Agroexport Crops in Costa Rica and Honduras (in jobs per year)

	Costa Rica Field	Packing	Total
Ornamental Plants[1]	3,002	1,863	4,865
Fruits	2,755	412	3,167
Vegetables[1]	1,340	540	1,880
Others	2,361	157	2,518
Total	9,458	2,972	12,430

	Honduras Field	Packing	Total
Ornamental Plants[1]	540	87	627
Fruits	5,967	364	6,331
Vegetables[1]	876	55	931
Others	3,588	410	3,998
Total	10,971	916	11,887

Notes: The dates for Honduras refer to 1991. The principal products in *Costa Rica* are: Ornamental Plants: flowers, foliage, ornamental plants, seeds; Fruits: pineapple, melon, strawberry, plantain; Vegetables: cassava, squash; Others: cacao, cardamon, macadamia, palm oil. In *Honduras*: Ornamental plants; Fruits: melon, orange, banana, grapefruit, pineapple; Vegetables: cucumber, squash; Others: cacao, palm oil, tabacco, cardamon, sesame.

NTAE production workers are female, according to 1991 estimates.[230] A survey of the NTAE labor force in Guatemala, Costa Rica, and Honduras showed that women occupy more than half the jobs associated with processing or post-harvest handling, and greenhouse cultivation.[231] (*See Table 10.*) In field labor, outside of greenhouses for NTAE cultivation, the percentage of women averages about 30 percent.[232] This proportion of women is much higher

Box 9. Women Workers in Ecuador's NTAEs

A survey of 120 women workers in NTAE businesses in Ecuador (80 on plantations and 40 in processing plants) was undertaken in late 1993 by the Centro de Planificación y Estudios Sociales, with support from the Universidad San Francisco de Quito and the World Resources Institute. Of the women surveyed, the majority were very young—in processing plants, 73 percent are under 24 years; on plantations, 60 percent are under 29 years and about half are single. Most of these women were using their earnings to supplement family income; the majority belonged to families with small subsistence farms (mostly under one hectare).

Some 70 percent of the women on plantations earned monthly wages between $33 (the minimum wage in 1992) and $67. In processing plants, monthly earnings for the majority ranged between $68 and $101. But managers rarely pay fixed salaries; payments vary, often based on a piece-work basis (for example, per bag of vegetables picked). In addition, 80 percent of the women on NTAE plantations and *all* of the women interviewed in processing plants frequently worked overtime; few were paid extra wages for this work, as legally required.

These workers lack basic labor rights and benefits. Of the 80 interviewed on plantations, 56 percent received none of the benefits specified in Ecuador's labor law, such as social security and health benefits; of the 40 women in the processing plants, 20 percent had no benefits. The law also requires that maternity leave be given with pay for three months before or after childbirth, and that women workers be given time off for nursing babies (15 minutes for each hour of work) for a year after birth. However, none of the women interviewed received this time off with pay. Furthermore, all lacked knowledge about their labor rights and benefits. A large majority—80 percent on plantations and 60 percent in processing plants—had no labor contract. Three months is the common duration of contracts for the few workers who have them. In most cases, a

Box 9. (continued)

job is established through an informal oral contract, making employees particularly vulnerable to unfair management practices.

Worker organizations or unions do not exist in the many NTAE companies included in this survey. NTAE owners emphasize that workers must not become involved in any such organization. Anybody caught trying to do so is fired. The majority of the women interviewed (58 percent on plantations and 60 percent in processing plants) think they have no possibility of advancing within their companies. Women's positions are low in the hierarchy; higher positions are reserved for men only.

The women generally spend their earnings on food, health, and children's education. The single women surveyed had slightly more varied expenses, but they also generally spent their earnings on meeting basic family needs. Most of these women maintained control of their own income. They reported that their earning power increased their self-confidence, respect from others, and decision-making influence in households. Most also said they were responsible as well for demanding domestic tasks and child care, which created physical pressures on top of the wage work.

In spite of problems, about 60 percent of those surveyed said they did not want to stop working in wage-earning jobs. However, the large majority (about 85 percent) said they would change jobs if it were possible. Many young single women said they would prefer to study so they could get better positions.

Source: Lucia Salamea, A. Mauro, M. Alameida, and M. Yepez. 1993. "Rol e Impacto en Mujeres Trabajadoras en Cultivos Notradicionales para la Exportación en Ecuador." Quito. CEPLAES/USFQ.

than in other agricultural sectors; for example, as an overall average, women account for only 6.3 percent of total agricultural labor in Costa Rica.[233]

Managers asked why women are increasingly employed in agroexports have provided several reasons. They generally say that women are more skilled at intricate tasks, including pruning, harvesting, sorting, selecting, and packaging, that require dexterity.[234] Studies by some firms have also shown that in this line of work women are more efficient and productive than men. One study of a rose plantation showed that the average female worker cut 4.5 flowers per minute, compared to 1.8 flowers per minute for males.[235] However, in many cases, managers' prefer to hire women because they are paid lower average wages than men for equivalent work, and have fewer opportunities for advancement and pay increases. Managers interviewed in a recent survey in Ecuador NTAE plantations mention that women are "more submissive, obedient, capable, and honest" workers than men;[236] this apparently gives managers a sense of more control. Surveys also reveal that most of the women employed are young, single, and childless. This is typical in many countries, partly because managers want to avoid paying for child-care and pregnancy leaves.[237]

In sum, numbers of jobs in NTAEs have increased substantially. But it is not enough to look at the numbers of jobs *per se*; wages and other labor conditions must also be examined.

3. Labor-related Constraints and Gender Concerns

Several labor-related problems are commonly found in NTAE production. Wage rates are one of the important concerns. Although comprehensive data is lacking, evidence from several areas shows that NTAE workers are often paid low, and sometimes unfair rates—below the minimum wage. In Guatemala, for example, the range of wages is $33 to $101 per month,[238] which is too low to cover most basic needs. In some unusual cases where the labor market is tight, NTAE managers have raised wages to attract women workers and pay more than traditional plantations do.[239]

Many jobs in this sector are insecure and sporadic, and workers tend to have unpredictable hours and very long working days during peak periods. In most of the NTAE-growing countries, a

91

high proportion of employees are temporary workers. For example, in Costa Rica and Honduras, over two thirds of the employees of fruit and vegetable NTAE farms and processing plants are temporary workers. This means that they lack job security and are subject to dismissal, especially during market declines. Studies in Paraguay and Chile show that growth in NTAE labor has tended to decline over time, particularly on larger-scale farms. In Chile, "wages in this [high-value fruit] sector have remained low and there is no evidence that this will change in the near future." [240] In the Central American countries, Costa Rica usually enforces labor laws somewhat better, whereas in Guatemala and Honduras, workers' rights to basic services and benefits are generally poorly protected.[241] Another concern noted frequently in the NTAE sector is the use of child labor. Although total numbers have not been recorded, children often work on NTAE farms, apparently more frequently than in other kinds of crops, and they inevitably miss school to do so.

In Ecuador, a recent field survey showed that a large majority of NTAE laborers lack legal contracts and employment benefits. Moreover, fluctuations in demand and supply of NTAE products mean that very few workers are required during particular phases of the growing season, especially in fruit and vegetable processing. During most of the year, processing plants operate below capacity and much of the labor force is idle. But when market demand is high—for instance, during holiday seasons for flower production—workers must work nights, weekends, and double-shifts, sometimes in violation of labor laws. In Guatemala, it has become common among smallholders to use the labor of children who would otherwise be in school.[242] Unions are usually prohibited or discouraged in the NTAE sector, which limits workers' bargaining potential. In Ecuador and Colombia, for example, if workers attempt to organize, they are usually admonished or fired.

For women workers, labor conditions in NTAEs present special problems.[243] (See Box 9.) Recent studies of plantations and processing plants show that women sometimes receive lower wages than men for similar work, toil for longer hours, and receive no extra pay for overtime hours. The large majority of these women face "double-day" demands; that is, after a full day's work in the fields or factories, women do unpaid household chores at home, with little help from men.[244] When women work double shifts during peak seasons, children must be left at home alone; few companies provide child care.[245]

Adverse labor conditions for women are particularly evident in Colombia's large flower industry. Here, a large proportion of workers are paid below minimum wage, live in very poor housing, and are subject to arbitrary wage cuts. Colombian flower workers are not allowed to join unions, so their basic labor rights are sometimes violated.[246] These problems have been serious enough to draw the attention of international human rights organizations who have pressured governments and businesses to improve working conditions and respect the law.

Health problems tend to be more serious for women than for men who work in NTAEs. Unprotected exposure to pesticides is one reason. *(See Section E.)* Also, in NTAE processing factories, as reported in Ecuador, many women who stand long hours on hard floors suffer from back and abdominal ailments.[247]

To make matters worse, women rarely get job promotions or salary increases in NTAE businesses, and extremely few women are managers or owners of NTAE companies. One major study of NTAEs in several countries found that "no major agribusinesses appeared to be owned and managed by women;" and only in Guatemala were there any—two in a sample of 22 small NTAE businesses.[248] This gender bias in NTAE ownership and management reflects historical patterns of discrimination: women have long been hindered by limited access to ownership of land, productive assets, and credit. But this imbalance is particularly incongruous in NTAEs since women do much of the marketing and processing work.

NTAE enterprises are not unique in illustrating these labor-related and gender concerns. Seasonality, irregular hours and job instability are also common in traditional plantations, serving both the export and domestic markets. Yet, these NTAE conditions deserve special attention, partly because this sector has been promoted as being socioeconomically beneficial, and partly because the instability and insecurity of the NTAE markets exacerbate the problems.

D. Dimensions of Diversification and Diversity

A popular expression advises against "putting all your eggs in one basket" and implies that diversification is generally advantageous, in many contexts. This has proven to be particularly true in agriculture, at both macroeconomic and farm levels.

The diversity of agricultural exports has increased significantly in countries that have embarked on NTAE strategies. In Ecuador, for instance, 124 kinds of non-traditional agricultural products were exported as of 1991.[249] These include not only well-known temperate crops, but exotic and eclectic products with very high value, such as shittake mushrooms, cashew oil, *araza* (a tropical fruit), amaranth, and macadamia nuts. Also included in specialty NTAEs are organic products grown by an increasing number of farmers. Particularly notable in this market is organic coffee (mainly from Mexico, Costa Rica, and Guatemala) and cocoa (from Bolivia). Unique tropical medicinal plants and spices that have been grown traditionally for local consumption are now also entering into niche export markets. This increasing diversity of products has been accompanied by the diversification of businesses, technologies, and skills.

At a national or regional level, diversification into NTAEs obviously reduces economic reliance on single traditional export commodities that have suffered price declines and helps offset fluctuations in markets.[250] At the farm level, diversification has similar advantages. From the consumers' perspective, diversification brings dietary benefits and a wider array of products to the market. In supermarkets in Northern cities, such as Washington D.C., more than 125 different fresh products are generally sold in the produce section; during winter months, more than one-third are imported.[251]

However, ironically, *diversification* into NTAEs at a national level often does *not* translate into crop *diversity* at a farm level. On the contrary, NTAE producers usually plant entire farms in monocultures, often from standardized foreign seeds. In Ecuador, only 30 percent of those surveyed rotate crops, and only 23 percent used intercropping; the percentages were even lower in the coastal areas.[252] Monocultures prevail in this context because of market demands, recommendations by technical advisors and

94

NTAE promoters, and economic efficiency considerations. For example, smallholders entering the NTAE market are often pressured to convert from planting mixed crops to growing a single export commodity.

Although monocultural systems can boost production efficiency and help fulfill market demands, farmers have realized that this uniform conversion often brings disadvantages. It increases agroecosystems' vulnerability to pests and diseases, as well as farmers' economic risks. Uniform exotic species introduced from temperate climates into the tropics are particularly susceptible to pests. For example, following the introduction of strawberries from Europe into Ecuador, the entire crop was wiped out in some areas during the second growing season, by a disease unknown to experts from several countries.[253] Producers bore major losses and had to switch to other varieties of berries.

Maintaining crop diversity *within* individual farms—whether in a given space (by intercropping) or over time (by crop rotation)—spreads risks, lowers vulnerability to fluctuating prices, reduces susceptibility to pests and diseases, and generally can help improve soil quality and nutrients. Planting legumes such as snow peas has additional agroecological value because these plants fix nitrogen in the soil, improving fertility. Such benefits of diversity are being recognized by small-scale farmers who have suffered losses by relying too heavily on NTAE monocultures, and even by some large agribusinesses that are successfully practicing crop rotation or intercropping.

Appreciating the benefits of diversification shows that the conventional concept of *comparative advantage* needs to be rethought, because it must shift from a focus on narrow specialization towards flexibility and diversity, which have proven to be important dimensions of comparative advantage. Nevertheless, these lessons have not been widely learned, and monocultures continue to predominate on most individual NTAE farms.

E. Impacts of Pesticide Use

As noted in Chapter 3, NTAE producers consistently use many types and high volumes of pesticides. In the short run, if they are used correctly, pesticides usually work rapidly and can reduce the risks of immediate losses and help ensure product quality. However, over time, pesticides also have a host of adverse impacts that impair productivity, health, and ecosystem functions, particularly when used inappropriately. Some of these effects jeopardize profits; others are external costs borne by society.

1. Direct Costs

Pesticides represent a significant proportion of total operating costs for NTAE production. Most are imported from industrial countries, which makes them expensive for developing nations. Studies consistently show that proportion of pesticide costs in most NTAEs matches or exceeds that of other crops (both export crops and produce for local markets).[254] These costs are particularly high in flower production, where pesticide use is intensive. On Ecuador's rose plantations, for instance, in one year an estimated average of 35 percent of operating costs was spent on agrochemicals, of which 85 percent was for fungicides and insecticides.[255] Nearly all chemicals are imported and tend to be high priced, even with tax exemptions. Studies in Guatemala have also documented high direct costs for pesticides. In the late 1980s the Consortium for International Crop Protection found that pesticide costs for melons had reached $735–$2,206 per hectare and had exceeded $2,206 per hectare for snow peas.[256] According to the study, pesticide purchases, application and technical assistance costs for NTAE vegetables accounted for 22.5 percent of total production costs. A recent study of pesticide use for snow peas in the Guatemalan highlands indicates that pesticide inputs are still very high, representing about 30 to 35 percent of costs for material inputs of production.[257] Another recent study showed that snow peas entail higher pesticide costs per hectare than either cotton or bananas, which formerly had the highest levels of pesticide use per unit of land.[258]

Substantial capital is obviously required for these chemicals, creating obstacles for producers, especially small-scale poor farmers who need credit to underwrite these costs. Moreover, these agrochemical costs have contributed to growing disparities in the distributional impacts of NTAEs.

2. Losses from Residues in Exported Foods

When pesticides are applied excessively or too close to harvest time, residues may accumulate in foods at levels that exceed the tolerance standards established by importing countries. Furthermore, the presence of *any* residues of certain unregistered pesticides is prohibited by regulatory agencies (such as the U.S. EPA) for specific crops. Because these residues pose health hazards to consumers, samples from shipments are inspected by government agencies, as noted in Chapter 1. When a violation is detected in the U.S. ports, the entire shipment is stopped and automatically detained, and the importer is required to test or have analyzed at least five future consecutive shipments at his/her own expense to ensure that residues are below the established tolerance level. In addition, the regulators increase the frequency of inspection, beyond the usual one percent sampling rate, for subsequent shipments of the same products. This leads to great financial losses to exporters and producers alike.[259]

These violations and detentions have proven to be a major problem affecting Latin American and Caribbean NTAE exports to the United States, as shown in Table 11. FDA data show that these pesticide-related detentions have occurred about *14,000 times* in the last decade for NTAE exporters from 10 countries of Latin America.[260] Economic losses totalled an estimated $95 million. Many of these problems have been associated with the "Dirty Dozen," highly toxic or persistent pesticides that are restricted or banned in the United States but continue to be exported and used in other countries. *(See Table 12.)* Violations are being detected in European ports as well. *(See Appendix 3 for more detailed data.)*

The most serious and frequent residue-detention problems have been in shipments from Guatemala and Mexico. During the late 1980s, detention rates for Guatemala's NTAEs reached 27.3 percent of the total shipments sampled.[261] Between 1990 and 1994, Guatemala's exports were detained 3,081 times because of residue violations, resulting in total losses of about $17,686,000.[262] Most of these detentions (1,755) occurred in 1993 alone, due almost entirely to the presence of chlorothalanil, a pesticide used in snow peas that is unregistered in the United States for this crop.[263] Following repeated violations, the Guatemalan government, in cooperation

Table 11. Summary of U.S. FDA Detentions for Pesticide Residues in Shipments of Fruits and Vegetables Imported from Selected Latin American and Caribbean Countries, FY 1984–94

	Total Number of Detentions[a]	Total Estimated Value of Shipments Detained ($US)[b]
Chile	666	$9,475,000
Colombia	79	200,000
Costa Rica	102	411,000
Dominican Republic	2,259	11,257,000
Ecuador	35	158,000
El Salvador	39	977,000
Guatemala	3,168	17,972,000
Honduras	66	269,000
Jamaica	150	583,000
Mexico	7,429	54,589,000

Source: WRI analysis of U.S. Food and Drug Administration data.

a. Shipments are detained for pesticide testing when a random sampling of a small portion of a shipment indicates potential violations of FDA regulations, or when a product from a certain country is under automatic detention, as is currently the case with snow peas from Guatemala and a handful of prod-

with U.S. government agencies, required that residue analyses be performed in Guatemala before shipment in addition to the usual import inspections, thus elevating the export costs.

Mexican export crops were detained 6,223 times in the 1980s, and 1,391 times in the 1990s, resulting in losses of $49.5 million and

Commonly Detained Products^c	Common Pesticides Causing Detention

Commonly Detained Products[c]	Common Pesticides Causing Detention
grapes, berries permethrins	
berries, naranjilla	chlorothalanil, methamidaphos
berries, chayote	chlorothalanil, methamidaphos
long beans, eggplant, peppers	monocrotophos, methamidaphos
strawberries, cantaloupe	chlorothalanil
okra	methamidaphos
snow peas, broccoli	chlorothalanil, methamidaphos
snow peas, okra	chlorothalanil, methamidaphos
peppers, papaya	monocrotophos, kelthane
peppers, strawberries, mangos	methamidaphos

ucts from the Dominican Republic. Many detained shipments are released for entry into the United States following testing.

b. Values are not exact due to possible minor inconsistencies or errors in measurement and calculation.

c. This list contains only some of the more common problem products and pesticides, though in most cases many more were involved.

$5.9 million respectively. The major residue problems here occurred in peppers, strawberries, and mangoes, and the principal pesticide involved was methamidophos, a toxic product with high health risks. Excessive residues have also been serious in NTAEs from the Dominican Republic; in 1987 and 1988, shipments with il-

Table 12. U.S. FDA Detentions for "Dirty Dozen" Pesticides in Shipments of Fruits and Vegetables from Latin America (FY 1983–94)[a]

	Mexico	Rest of Latin America[b]	Total Number
1983	parathion(1) endrin (1)	heptachlor (2)	4
1984	endrin (7) DDT (14) lindane (31) parathion (1)	——	53
1985	lindane (2) heptachlor (1) endrin (2)	——	5
1986	endrin (4) parathion (2) lindane (1)	chlordane (1)	8
1987	endrin (1) DDT (7) lindane (11) EDB (918) parathion (13)	——	950
1988	EDB (2) heptachlor (1) DDT (60) endrin (1) lindane (20) parathion (12) chlordane (1)	parathion (1) dieldrin (3)	101

Table 12. (continued)

	Mexico	Rest of Latin America[b]	Total Number
1989	parathion (14) lindane (27) DDT (35) heptachlor (3) EDB (1)	aldrin (2) EDB (1)	83
1990	lindane (28) DDT (7) parathion (1)	parathion (1) EDB (49) lindane (1)	87
1991	lindane (12) DDT (3)	parathion (11) EDB (3)	29
1992	lindane (9) DDT (1)	parathion (1) EDB (7) heptachlor (4) chlordane (1)	23
1993	lindane (3) heptachlor (1)	heptachlor (29) chlordane (1) lindane (1)	35
1994	DDT (1) heptachlor (1) DBCP (1)	lindane (1)	4

Source: WRI analysis of U.S. Food and Drug Administration data.
Notes:
a. Only through February, 1994.
b. Includes Chile, Costa Rica, Dominican Republic, Guatemala, and Jamaica.

legal residues far exceeded those from other countries and 12.2 percent of the samples violated U.S. government standards.[264] In 1989, losses totalled $2.5 million from residue violations.[265] These problems were particularly serious in oriental vegetables: in 1988, several growers reported residue-related losses of hundreds of thousands of dollars in a single month. The FDA subsequently imposed automatic detentions on five vegetables, requiring exporters to pay an additional charge of $400 for each cargo container tested in the United States.[266]

In contrast, some countries have experienced few problems or losses so far from pesticide residues in NTAEs. Ecuador's exports, for example, have been detained only 30 times in U.S. markets since 1985, largely because Ecuador's NTAE sector is still relatively new and small. Nevertheless, producers, exporters, and importers have become increasingly concerned about these regulations and the risks will probably grow more serious as NTAEs expand under present production practices. Poorer farmers suffer more than wealthier producers when crops are detained because it is more difficult for them to recover from losses and to respond to regulatory imperatives.[267]

Pesticides used in NTAEs also damage the environment and pose risks to local crops thereby raising costs for producers and for society in general. One chemical of particular concern is methyl bromide, a fumigant used extensively for most NTAEs, in both the production and marketing processes. Although effective and economical for these purposes, methyl bromide is highly toxic to workers and contributes to the destruction of the Earth's protective ozone layer in the upper atmosphere. *(See Box 10.)* Moreover, water pollution has been cited as resulting from pesticides and fertilizers used in NTAE production.[268] However, the extent of NTAE-related contamination has not been monitored systematically, partly because of technological limitations.

3. Resistance and the Self-Defeating "Pesticide Treadmill"

When pesticides are used continually and intensively over time, pests evolve capacities to tolerate the chemicals. This pest resistance is often accompanied by the death of natural enemies and outbreaks of secondary pests. Consequently, chemicals lose effec-

Box 10. Controversy over Methyl Bromide in Export Agriculture

Methyl bromide is a chemical used extensively to fumigate soil, food, and non-food commodities. It is one of the most widely used fumigants in the world, mainly because it is relatively inexpensive and is highly effective in killing all organisms it contacts. It is also colorless and odorless, which contributes to its popularity. In most countries, methyl bromide is used in agriculture to fumigate soils before planting and to disinfect food commodities before and during transport and marketing. Although it is used on all kinds of crops, the largest share of methyl bromide used worldwide is in intensive high-value monoculture production and marketing processes, particularly for export-oriented cash crops.

The use of this chemical is particularly significant in export crops in Latin America and the Caribbean. In most NTAEs, methyl bromide is used heavily and in growing volumes, especially for fumigating perishable fruits and vegetables to fulfill quarantine regulations. In fact, import laws and requirements in the North force exporting countries to use methyl bromide on food commodities and flowers, even if alternatives exist for sanitation procedures.

Although methyl bromide has benefits, it has alarming disadvantages and costs. The U.S. Environmental Protection Agency (EPA) has classified this chemical as a Category I acute toxin—among the most dangerous toxic substances. At low levels, if inhaled or absorbed through the skin, it can cause symptoms ranging from chest pain to lung congestion. It can also lead to neurological problems, such as headaches, nausea, and visual abnormalities. Exposure to slightly higher levels of the product can lead to seizures or even death hours or days after exposure. Workers face the greatest risk of exposure and injury. Records of these problems are highly deficient in Latin America, mainly because of lack of familiarity with the symptoms; but in California, methyl bromide ranked eighth as a cause of acute illnesses from pesticides.

Box 10. (continued)

The product also has significant long-term effects. Extended exposure has led to impaired motor coordination, muscle aches, and chronic fatigue among farmworkers. Evidence from animal studies suggests that methyl bromide is a reproductive toxin and may cause cancer and harm immune-system and hormonal functions.

Precautions, such as wearing masks or protective clothing, are seldom taken in Latin America. Yet even if they are, workers cannot fully avoid the hazards of methyl bromide during preparation and applications. The common types of fumigation practices permit the methyl bromide vapors to escape into the air and to be inhaled by workers.

Methyl bromide also destroys the ozone layer in the upper atmosphere, which protects organisms from dangerous levels of ultraviolet solar radiation. The United Nations Environment Programme reports that methyl bromide has caused 5 to 10 percent of current worldwide ozone depletion. Ozone depletion has been linked to increased incidence of skin cancer, cataracts, and immune-system depression. The dangers of methyl bromide have raised considerable alarm and opposition within government agencies (such as the U.S. Environmental Protection Agency) and by many other groups concerned about environmental and social issues. In 1993, the EPA recommended regulatory action to ban production and use of this product within seven years. The Agency categorized it as a "Class I" product (i.e, most potent) among ozone-depleters. The Clean Air Act of the United States also calls for a ban on methyl bromide in the U.S. in 2001.

However, the USDA and many agribusinesses vehemently oppose such proposed legislation, arguing that a ban on methyl bromide would seriously harm national economies and their businesses. Although alternatives exist and are already used by innovative farmers and pest control companies, most industries in this business resist the efforts to phase out methyl

Box 10. (continued)

bromide, thus thwarting reform. Indeed, methyl bromide is exempted from labelling requirements and an excise tax that is imposed on other Class I ozone-depleting chemicals.

In Latin America, NTAE promoters and producers also strongly oppose a ban on methyl bromide. Managers of export companies and of NTAE projects fear catastrophe without this pesticide; they assert that such a phase-out would mean economic failure for the NTAE companies, making exporters unable to comply with the quarantine and sanitary regulations required by importing nations. Indeed, the contradictory demands from USDA and EPA do pose serious dilemmas for exporters. However, some countries have already banned or regulated methyl bromide. In 1992, the Netherlands banned use of this product for all soil fumigation. In 1985, Germany prohibited its use on food crops and in 1989 restricted its use on non-food crops. These countries, and increasing numbers of producers, are realizing that the costs are not worth it, and that non-chemical alternatives can pay off. Some of the important effective alternative methods include crop rotation, the use of pest-resistant plant varieties, cover crops, heat treatments, reliance on composts and manures, and addition of "soil amendments" that enhance beneficial soil microorganisms.

Ceasing dependency on methyl bromide in NTAEs, as in many other crops, can help lead to more sustainable and safe food systems. In addition, changes in regulatory policies are needed to induce the transition. The U.S. government, for example, could adjust the USDA's quarantine requirements and phytosanitary standards for produce from the developing countries, to ensure more consistency with EPA policies and to reduce the obligations to use methyl bromide. At the international level, in 1995, government bodies involved in an international treaty on ozone (the Montreal Protocol) will consider regulations that could restrict methyl bromide. The multilateral ozone fund should provide assistance to help Latin Amer-

---

Box 10. (continued)

ican producers and other enterprises worldwide meet the costs of the transition to more sustainable alternatives.

Sources: World Health Organization, 1991. *International Programme on Chemical Safety and Health Criteria for Methyl Bromide.* Geneva: WHO; U.S. Environmental Protection Agency. 1986. *Pesticide Fact Sheet: Methyl Bromide.* Washington, D.C. USEPA; Clark Chip, et al, 1994, "Southern Exposure: the phaseout of methyl bromide in developing countries," San Francisco: Pesticide Action Network and Methyl Bromide Alternatives Network, 1994. Briefing Kit.

---

tiveness in pest control, and high economic losses ensue. Farmers then become trapped into increasing pesticide inputs to try to regain control, creating a vicious circle known as the "pesticide treadmill." The process is accelerated if pesticides are used excessively or if one product is used season after season. This predicament has affected many agroexport crops in Latin America, and has led to major losses, particularly in cotton and bananas.[269]

The heavy use of pesticides in NTAEs has contributed to a major problem of resistance and resurgence of whiteflies in Latin America and the Caribbean, reaching crisis proportions in some areas.[270] The pesticide-resistant whiteflies are also transmitting serious viruses that have seriously damaged NTAE crops in Chile, Brazil, and Argentina. More than one million hectares of cropland in South America has been abandoned due to these viruses.[271] In Honduras, outbreaks of resistant whiteflies and leaf miners reached crisis proportions in the late 1980s, reducing melon harvests by 45 to 56 percent in the Choluteca region.[272] As a result, some melon producers lost their entire crop. Such losses particularly devastated small producers, forcing them out of competition. Specialists identified frequent pesticide applications and recommendations of pesticide salesmen as the main sources of the problems.[273]

In the Dominican Republic, the Constanza Valley vegetable-growing region suffered major damage from an explosive outbreak of greenhouse whiteflies (*Trialeurodes vaporariorum*) that had become highly resistant due to excessive pesticide use in the 1980's.[274] Tomato and melon producers in the Azua Valley were plagued by a major outbreak of the resistant cotton whitefly (*Bemisa tabaci*) that resulted in a 59 percent reduction of tomato exports, a loss of $5.9 million, and a 48 percent decline in the area planted in tomatoes.[275] Here too, producers later realized that excessive chemical applications provoked the problems. Throughout Latin America and the Caribbean, the resistant whiteflies are now nearly impossible to control by chemical means.[276]

As more land is planted in export-oriented vegetable crops, new viruses appear because most of these crops enhance the development of large insect vector populations. For example, tomatoes have served as breeding hosts for whiteflies (*B. tabaci*), compounding the spread of whitefly-borne viruses throughout Central America and Mexico.[277]

So far, in Ecuador, where the NTAE boom is just beginning and detection is more difficult, very few producers have reported serious problems from pest resistance or major pest outbreaks in these crops. But on traditional export plantations, resistance is rarely recognized until it reaches crisis proportions and results in major economic losses. In Ecuador, there may be an opportunity to reduce pesticide use and develop alternative methods *before* the problem escalates.

4. Health Hazards

With the heavy and growing use of pesticides in NTAEs, ever more people are being exposed to toxic chemicals, and there are increasing numbers of acute poisonings and chronic health problems. Most victims are agricultural workers—the poorest people involved in NTAE production. Usually provoked by direct exposure to toxins, acute poisonings can bring on vomiting, fever, vertigo, diarrhea, delirium, muscular convulsions, neural damage, or even death. The number of acute poisonings in the NTAE sector is not known, but descriptions from farmworkers surveyed provide evidence of some cases. Chronic effects include headaches, allergies, dizziness, dermatitis, blurred vision, or, in the longer-term, carcinogenic disorders. In a survey of workers in Ecuador, 62 percent said they had suffered health problems from exposure to pesticides while working. Of these, almost 25 percent had experienced more than three symptoms; 36.5 percent experienced two to three symptoms, while the remaining 10.5 percent had single persistent symptoms, such as headaches.[278] Many workers show clinical signs of exposure to toxins.[279]

Health hazards are particularly serious in flower production, especially in Colombia and Ecuador, partly because toxic nematicides such as aldicarb and fenamifos are heavily used. *(See Box 11.)* Although aldicarb was banned in Ecuador in late 1991, it was still used as late as 1993 because flower growers value its efficacy more than worker safety. Also, managers commonly allow unprotected workers to continue working alongside workers applying chemicals. [280]

These health impacts have also lowered workers' productivity throughout the region. Many victims need intensive medical treatment that they can neither get nor afford. Women are particularly vulnerable to both acute poisonings and long-term damage from exposure to pesticides.[281] Although growing attention is being given to these health issues, the problems have not been resolved, given present patterns in agrochemical use.

With the combination of these adverse effects, pesticide use can be self-defeating. Were the costs of this use fully incorporated into farm accounting, the economic returns from pesticides would be unfavorable in many cases.

F. Other Environmental Impacts: Changes in Land Use

How has NTAE growth affected natural resources, particularly land, vegetation, and water? Comprehensive assessments are not available, but preliminary appraisals suggest that NTAEs cause significant environmental concerns. Areas of forest cover have been cleared for NTAEs in a few areas; for example, an estimated 3000 hectares of forested land in Costa Rica has been cleared for citrus farms.[282] In the Guatemalan highlands, the expansion of NTAE vegetables on to steeply sloped hillsides has caused some defor-

Box 11. Behind the Rosy Harvests: Risks to Women Workers' Health on Flower Farms

The female labor force is the backbone of the export flower industry in Latin America. Accounting for 70 to 80 percent of laborers on the flower plantations of Ecuador and Colombia, these women toil to keep production up. Ironically, however, their own well-being is often jeopardized.

Worker health is strongly influenced by several basic factors, including wages and job stability, the work environment, housing conditions, diet, and public health and education services. Most of these conditions are not provided or are inadequate on export flower plantations. The workers are exposed to hazards from agrochemicals, and their legal rights to safe work conditions are often violated. Consequently, they suffer from a myriad of health impairments, stemming mainly from high exposure to toxic pesticides. In particular, the closed warm environment in greenhouses compounds the build-up of toxic vapors and aggravates the dangers of exposure.

In Ecuador, a 1993 study of 80 women working on flower plantations and other NTAE farms revealed heavy use of organophosphates, carbamates, and piretrinas, including some banned products. This study, supported by the World Resources Institute, found a high incidence of blurred vision, intolerance to light, headaches, and nausea among the workers—all symptoms associated with excessive exposure to organophosphates and carbamates. Nearly two thirds (62 percent) of the plantation workers interviewed are obligated to continue working while pesticides are being applied; and this group experiences the most ill effects. Furthermore, the majority of women workers receive no training or information on pesticide use, much less protective equipment. Some 40 percent of the workers interviewed had no protection and the rest occasionally received gloves, boots, and rarely, glasses. Even where women were given protective equipment, those "safety" measures (masks, gloves, etc.) were inadequate or poorly maintained. The services and infrastructure for health and

Box 11. (continued)

hygiene are also deficient on these plantations, which aggravates these health risks. Only 5 percent of the workers interviewed received medical examinations paid for by the companies.

In Colombia, conditions are similar, yet probably more serious, partly because the scale is multiplied. A study of a population of 8,867 workers on flower plantations near Bogotá showed that they were exposed to 127 different types of pesticides. The main pesticides include Temik, Captan, Dithane, Daconil, Methyl Parathion, Phosdrin, and Thiodan. Three of these are considered extremely toxic by the World Health Organization. An estimated 20 percent of the pesticides used in Colombia's flowers are banned or not registered in the U.K or the U.S. Captan has been prohibited for use in Germany because of its carcinogenic effects, and Temik has been prohibited in the United States because of its extreme toxicity. Yet, such products continue to be exported and purchased by flower companies.

Although men usually apply these chemicals, female laborers work in chemical-laden conditions. Managers usually send the workers to the fields (greenhouses) immediately after pesticide applications, violating the technical requirements for re-entry intervals. Women workers have consequently experienced acute and chronic effects. In Colombia, nearly two thirds of the workers suffer from headaches, nausea, impaired vision, conjunctivitis, rashes, and asthma. They also suffer serious longer-term insidious effects, such as stillbirths, miscarriages, and respiratory and neurological problems. A comprehensive scientific study published in 1990 on occupational health conditions showed that female workers experienced a moderate increase in the prevalence of spontaneous abortion, premature births, and children with congenital malformations after working in floriculture, compared to the incidence before starting work on these plantations.

Box 11. (continued)

Pressures from strict management systems exacerbate these problems. Pushed to maximize output and speed, workers are treated like inanimate and expendable factors of production by many plantation owners, partly because replacement workers are generally easy to find in the rural areas. Inadequate or below-minimum wages, poor living conditions, and lack of respect for the laws governing maternity leave are common. In both Colombia and Ecuador, women have tried to organize themselves to address these problems and to assert their rights, but plantation managers usually respond with reprimands, penalties, and dismissals.

Some flower farms have improved occupational health conditions to some extent, partly in response to negative media attention and pressure by workers and environmental NGOs. In both Ecuador and Colombia, for example, several flower companies now take workers' blood samples to check for hazards, and some have improved medical services and provide masks and gloves for workers. Yet, many flower producers are not taking such steps, and more changes are urgently needed on all farms to prevent and mitigate these hazards.

Sources: For Ecuador: Raul Harari, 1994. "Mujer, condiciones, y medio ambiente de trabajo en las plantaciones y procesadoras de cultivos notradicionales de exportación." Draft report. (Quito: Universidad San Francisco de Quito and World Resources Institute, 1994.) *For Colombia:* FENSUAGRO, "Cuando las flores hablan," *Profamilia,* Octubre 13–14. Flower News. 1993; "Women flower workers to visit for Colombia Human Rights Network." Washington, D.C. *Colombia Human Rights Network;* Mauricio Restrepo, et al. "Prevalence of adverse reproductive outcomes in a population occupationally exposed to pesticides in Colombia," *Scandinavia Journal of Work Environmental Health.* Vol 6, 1990. pp. 232–238; Jorg Jenrich, 1992. "Flower News," Stuttgart: Bread for the World; CUT. 1991.

estation[283] and pushed subsistence production into previously forested areas[284] but total area is not certain. These deforested areas have been subject to soil erosion and declining yields. So far, however, deforestation for NTAEs is not as serious as it is in traditional export plantations, which in many countries created extensive clearing of forests.

The use of chemical fertilizers for NTAEs, like the use of pesticides, is widespread and heavy. Fertilizers can yield important benefits to production when applied correctly; but the excessive use of chemical fertilizers has reportedly led to water pollution from runoff in some areas,[285] though how often is unknown. Repeated inputs of fertilizers can also lead to soil toxicity in the long run, resulting in fertility loss. As with pesticides, farmers tend to use chemical soil supplements intensively in continuous monocultural systems to boost short-term profitability, at the expense of long-term sustainability.

One of the most notable and serious environmental impacts in current export production is the massive destruction of mangroves caused by the growth of the shrimp industry, first in Ecuador (where shrimp is now considered a traditional export) and now in Honduras, where shrimp is still seen as an NTAE.[286] Mangroves are mainly threatened by the residues from algae-forming fertilizers used in shrimp food. Systematic measurements of NTAE-related soil erosion have not been completed, but erosion is observable, particularly on steep slopes. In Guatemala, snow pea producers have consistently reported declining yields over time that are partly attributable to soil erosion in areas cultivated year after year. The level of erosion depends partly on the crop type, and on the land-use practices.

Perennial fruit trees, vines, and bushes can help provide soil protection and water retention, compared with other types of annual crops.[287] Perennial fruit trees are especially advantageous when intercropped, as in agroforestry systems. However, agroforestry is rarely found in NTAEs since the large majority of NTAE farms are planted in monocultures. The predominance of uniform varieties increases agroecological and economic risks, narrows the genetic base, and displaces diverse indigenous varieties of crops and vegetation, further undermining sustainability.

G. Additional Socioeconomic Challenges

NTAE producers face additional challenges besides the economic impediments mentioned. Decision-makers in this sector stress the difficulties of inadequate post-harvest transport systems, lack of refrigerated storage, weak technical services, and lack of access to market information. Most producers cannot easily improve these capacities without external assistance. Coupled with complex importer demands and market fluctuations, these factors are particularly daunting for poor smallholders trying to enter and succeed in the non-traditional sector. Such impediments raise questions about institutional and technical capacities for sustaining NTAE production and marketing. Indeed, given the many uncertainties discussed in this chapter and elsewhere, one NTAE program official called NTAE production "legal gambling."[288]

In sum, while some elements of non-traditional agroexport growth are promising, many socioeconomic and environmental disadvantages elevate costs and call into question the sustainability and equity of the strategy. The assessment of opportunities and problems, using a lens of sustainable development, shows the need to integrate concerns about environmental and social soundness and long-term economic security into agricultural development policies.

V.
AVOIDING ADVERSE EFFECTS AND INCREASING BENEFITS OF NTAES

Initiatives are being taken in a few countries to address some of the environmental, social, and economic problems of NTAes. Generally such attempts respond to serious problems; only rarely are they preventive strategies. These alternative efforts by public and private agencies as well as individual producers, take many forms, as summarized in this chapter.

A. Financial Sustainability

Achieving economic sustainability means in part strengthening market development. Thus, NTAE trade associations and programs have increased efforts aimed at improving business management training, market information services, technical advice, credit access, and, in some cases, infrastructure and transport systems for NTAE markets. USAID has supported these activities, but now these projects have to sustain themselves and many are becoming privatized, as the Agency dramatically reduces its financial assistance to NTAEs in Latin America. For some businesses, this shift is not likely to hinder entrepreneurial capabilities, but for smaller, less capitalized producers, such economic risk factors as access to credit and exchange rate policies represent serious constraints that often exclude them altogether from the potential advantages of NTAEs. Improving long-term financial sustainability of NTAE growth also depends on stability of exchange rates and monetary and fiscal policies, as well as trade negotiations—factors which are clearly difficult to stabilize and to predict. (Examining the present and potential attempts to reform such economic policies is beyond the scope of this analysis.)

B. Addressing Pesticide Impacts—IPM and Pesticide Regulations

Several institutions and producers are responding to the environmental impacts of NTAEs, especially pesticide-related problems. Guatemala and Honduras have reduced pesticide use notably and begun to develop integrated pest management programs. In Guatemala, serious losses from residue-related detentions in vegetables, especially snow peas, sparked several initiatives in the early 1990s aimed at rationalizing pesticide use, primarily to stop the use of unregistered chemicals, and to help improve phytosanitary conditions. Several of these efforts have been carried out under the umbrella of the Agricultural Development Project (PDA), which was financed by USAID, coordinated by the Ministry of Agriculture, and involved other institutions and the private sector.

An important effort in Guatemala, initiated in 1991, was a Highlands Agricultural Development project, which focussed mainly on Integrated Pest Management (IPM) research for snow peas and also included work on tomatoes, broccoli and other vegetables. In this project, several research and development institutions collaborated with the private sector and USAID to carry out IPM research and then undertake outreach and technology transfer. *(See Box 12.)*

Another initiative in Guatemala was the creation of the Integral Program for Agricultural and Environmental Protection (PIPPA), which tries to reduce pesticide residue problems and to promote compliance with pesticide and sanitary standards in NTAEs (especially for snow peas). PIPPA works with U.S. government agencies and trade associations to provide technical services and to develop laboratory capacities for residue analysis. The National Committee for Snow Peas also concentrates on pesticide residue problems. The international pesticide trade association (GIFAP) has undertaken a three-year program in Guatemala on general pesticide safety and management training, with educational materials and training

Box 12. IPM Initiatives in Guatemalan Snow Peas

Repeated problems of pesticide-residue detentions in Guatemala's snow pea exports led to major crises. Although several types of Guatemala's vegetable exports were rejected due to residue violations, snow peas met this fate thousands of times in the early 1990s. Repeated failures prompted a significant effort to develop alternatives to chemical-intensive production.

One major response was the project on Integrated Pest Management (IPM) in snow peas and other NTAE vegetables. Launched in 1991, the research and development process for this project involved the collaboration of several institutions, including the Plant Protection unit of the National Agricultural Research Center (ICTA), the Agricultural Center for Tropical Research and Training (CATIE), and the Agricultural Research Fund (ARF), as well as the Snow Pea Trade Association, USAID, and the Agrochemical Association for some aspects. The objectives were to research and apply integrated pest and pesticide management methods and to reduce pesticide inputs and detentions.

The project scientists began with two years of research on the main pest and disease problems related to snow peas. On this basis, the team generated new alternatives for IPM, including solarization, the use of plastic "traps," the destruction of crop residues, crop rotation, and the rational use of pesticides with EPA registration. Most of these methods are profitable and simple to apply using locally available resources. The project also included training and technical assistance for the personnel of export companies, chemical salesmen, farm managers, and both small and large farmers. Activities included short courses on IPM and demonstration field days for producers, packers, and technicians from chemical companies. During 1992, the team worked mainly with snow pea producers and exporters, providing short training seminars to 201 technicians, 992 smallholders, 47 representatives of agroexport companies, and 19 chemical salesmen.

Box 12. (continued)

In late 1993, an assessment was undertaken to identify the impacts of efforts to introduce IPM in snow peas in Chimaltenango and Sacatapequez, Guatemala's major snow-pea producing areas. A main objective was to determine whether farmers and technical personnel were adopting IPM methods and learning about and avoiding pesticide problems in snow peas. An interdisciplinary team, from both CEMAT, an NGO working on Appropriate Technology, and ICTA, the National Agricultural Research Center, carried out the study, with support from the World Resources Institute, Management Systems International, and USAID.

This study involved surveys in about 30 *aldeas* (villages) and 19 municipalities, along with a participatory workshop among small producers. The results, summarized in Table 13, showed that most farmers surveyed have adopted at least some of the IPM practices, and about half are following pesticide residue precautions. However, a few of the key recommended practices, particularly use of sticky plastic-bag insect traps, solarization, and tilling before planting were adopted by fewer than 10 percent of the farmers interviewed. Furthermore, unregistered pesticides were still being used in 57 cases. The main reasons given by farmers for deciding not to adopt certain techniques were a lack of knowledge of the methods, insufficient time, and high expense. Another possible problem was that project technicians rarely used participatory approaches for technology transfer; and the conventional top-down approach they used is usually less effective for inducing changes.

In sum, these findings suggest that some useful initiatives are being made to reduce pesticide costs, but that much more work is needed to transform production practices.

Source: Richard Fisher, R. Cáceres, E. Cáceres, D. Ardon. Informe Final (borrador), Evaluación de Manejo de plagas y Plaguicidas en Arveja China del Altiplano de Guatemala. Guatemala: CEMAT/ICTA/WRI, 1994.

courses for technical people at all levels. Other groups, such as the Peace Corps in tandem with the Panamerican Agricultural School (El Zamorano), are also undertaking programs to reduce pesticide hazards, though these are not focussed only on NTAEs. These activities have positive aims and some have had beneficial results. Residue detentions declined considerably between 1992 and 1994, suggesting that farmers are at least learning to curtail the use of unregistered pesticides. As far as impacts of IPM programs are concerned, a few assessments have been undertaken. In particular, one comprehensive study of smallholders assessed the adoption and impacts of Integrated Pest Management (IPM) methods in snow peas.[289] *(See Box 12 and Table 13.)* This original study also analyzed the economic viability of IPM, and showed that, generally, net returns are greater in snow pea production that uses a full array of IPM methods compared to yields in conventional chemical-intensive production systems. *(See Tables 14A and 14B.)* Similarly, studies in broccoli and tomato production showed similar economic advantages of IPM over conventional pest control methods.

In Honduras, IPM has been successfully implemented in melon production through a collaborative project. El Zamorano, CATIE, the Ministry of Agriculture, and such NGOs as World Neighbors have worked with melon growers to test and apply effective pest control methods. The effort, which featured a participatory approach resulted in an adoption rate of IPM techniques that was higher than expected, and in a significant reduction of the pest and pesticide problems that were plaguing melon producers.[290]

In Ecuador, the export promotion program, PROEXANT, with support from USAID, has carried out some activities for plant protection and pesticide/pest management, including training seminars on pesticide precautions, studies on pests and pesticide use patterns, and experiments on biological control methods in NTAEs. In 1992–93, for example, PROEXANT gave dozens of short seminars on pesticide management. Non-government organizations, such as Fundación Natura, have called public attention to problems in NTAE plantations, especially in flower farms, and have carried out monitoring and advised producers. Although Ecuador's initial steps are important, they receive much less fund-

Table 13. Adoption/Use of Integrated Pest Management Methods in Snow Peas: Results of Survey Among Smallholders in Guatemala

Practice	Number (n=124)	Percent
Put up stakes before planting	10	8.1
Fertilization before planting	119	96.0
Put up twine before planting	8	6.5
Liming	29	23.4
Analyze soil	25	20.2
Use certified seed	114	91.9
Solarization	4	3.2
Plant in raised beds	60	48.4
Disinfect soils against fungus	76	61.3
Use organic fertilizer	97	78.2
Apply insecticides to soil	70	56.5
Use authorized pesticides	112	90.3
Know proper application equipment	96	77.4
Calibrate equipment	46	37.1
Use protective equipment	46	37.1
Apply by calendar	88	71.0
Sample/monitor pests	64	51.6
Apply pesticide based on monitoring	58	46.8
Use biological insecticides	40	32.3
Use nitrate as source of nitrogen	22	17.7
Use 12-15 levels of twine (staking)	17	13.7
At least two weedings	124	100.0
Intercropping	33	26.6
Selection of spray nozzles	44	35.5
Use of plastic-bag traps	11	8.9
Rotate pesticides	103	83.1
Use 6–11 levels of twine (staking)	101	81.5
Destroy crop residues	77	62.1

Source: WRI/CEMAT/ICTA survey, 1994, producers in Chimaltenango and Sacatapequez, Guatemala.

Table 14A. Cost Analysis of Conventional Cultivation of Snow Peas, Broccoli and Tomatoes in Guatemala (prices in Quetzales/ha.)

	Snow Peas	Broccoli	Tomatoes
Total Costs	**18,713.49**	**8,660.33**	**16,485.97**
Direct Costs	14,028.10	6,492.00	12,358.30
Land rent	320.00	320.00	320.00
Nursery			
preparation		308.00	168.00
Soil preparation	308.00	308.00	308.00
Transplanting		224.00	224.00
Disinfection	126.00		
Planting	140.00		
Cultivation tasks			
fertilizing	112.00	126.00	168.00
weeding/tilling	756.00	924.00	924.00
staking	252.00		168.00
tying cord			168.00
apply pesticides	350.00	224.00	308.00
trellising	350.00		
Harvest			
cutting/classifying	2,760.00	252.00	308.00
transport		126.00	
Inputs			
fertilizers	680.00	1,755.00	1,224.00
insecticides	1,224.00	720.00	2,520.00
fungicides	2,250.00	800.00	1,800.00
seeds	2,250.00	135.00	960.00
bamboo stakes	1,350.00		300.00
plastic cord	800.10		2,490.30
Transportation		270.00	
Indirect Costs	4,685.39	2,168.33	4,127.67
Gross Revenue	**42,000.00**	**14,040.00**	**24,000.00**
Net Revenue	**23,286.51**	**5,379.67**	**7,514.03**
Profit as % of			
Investment	**124.44**	**62.12**	**45.58**

Table 14B. Cost Analysis of IPM Cultivation of Snow Peas, Broccoli and Tomatoes in Guatemala (prices in Quetzales/ha.)

	Snow Peas	Broccoli	Tomatoes
Total Costs	**17,119.36**	**7,953.31**	**14,080.67**
Direct Costs	12,833.10	5,962.00	10,555.22
Land rent	320.00	320.00	320.00
Establishment of barriers			28.00
Nursery preparation		308.00	168.00
Soil preparation	308.00	308.00	308.00
Transplanting		224.00	224.00
Disinfection	126.00		
Planting	140.00		
Cultivation tasks			
fertilizing	112.00	126.00	168.00
weeding/tilling	756.00	924.00	924.00
staking	168.00		252.00
placement of cord			168.00
applying pesticides	224.00	112.00	126.00
trellising	350.00		
destroying residues	42.00	42.00	
placing of traps	28.00		42.00
Harvest			
cutting/classifying	2,760.00	252.00	308.00
transport		126.00	
Inputs			
fertilizers	680.00	1,755.00	1,224.00
insecticides	935.00	660.00	1,470.00
fungicides	1,400.00	400.00	900.00
seeds	2,250.00	135.00	960.00
bamboo stakes	1,350.00		300.00
plastic cord	800.10		2,490.30
plastic bags	156.75		156.75
vaseline	102.17		102.17
Transportation		270.00	
Indirect Costs	4,286.26	1,991.31	3,525.44
Gross Revenue	**42,000.00**	**14,040.00**	**24,000.00**
Net Revenue	**24,880.64**	**6,086.69**	**9,919.33**
Profit as % of			
Investment	**145.34**	**76.53**	**70.45**

Source: USAID/G. MAD, unpublished data from field study in Guatemala), University of Missouri, 1994

ing support than the Guatemalan programs. Moreover, Ecuador producers have done very little to implement IPM in non-traditional crops; only a few biological control research efforts (by private companies such as Latenreco) and a few experimental applications have been undertaken.

Another significant initiative throughout the region is the involvement of United States government agencies, particularly the Animal and Plant Health Inspection Service (APHIS), to help address pesticide problems. APHIS is assisting export-promotion projects and Ministries of Agriculture to help monitor residues, investigate sources of problems, and identify alternatives. APHIS has also helped the Ministries to set up new laboratory testing facilities. The USDA, FDA, and EPA also regularly send information to the NTAE projects. These efforts are contributing to improvements in pesticide and pest management in some areas, even though problems continue to grow elsewhere.

C. Organic Production: Promising Green Markets

The development of organic production among smallholders is an innovative and effective way to increase the socioeconomic benefits of NTAES and to avoid adverse environmental impacts. Demand for organic products is growing rapidly in Northern markets, and production in Latin America is burgeoning. For example, the U.S. market for organic products grew annually by 14 percent between 1988 and 1992; and USDA projections show that it will grow to more than 10 percent per year in the future.[291] Moreover, prices for organic products are from 40 to 70 percent higher than those for non-organic crops in the United States.[292]

To serve new "green" markets, successful organic NTAE enterprises that have emerged in a few cases, mainly in Bolivia, Mexico, El Salvador, and Costa Rica, can be particularly beneficial to poor smallholders. A notable Bolivian example is a large federation of small farmers, called the El Ceibo cooperative, that produces and markets organic cacao for European and North American markets. *(See Box 13.)* El Ceibo also manufactures its own chocolate products, adding value that is returned to native producers. The federation is made up of 37 agricultural co-ops with 900 members; an-

Box 13. A Unique Chocolate and Traditional Organization in Bolivia

Deep in the interior tropical region of Bolivia, indigenous farmers of the El Ceibo Cooperative can be found working year round in the cultivation of organic cocoa, which—once processed and packaged—is destined for export to Western Europe and health food stores in the United States. El Ceibo consists of 37 smaller co-ops (about 900 members) that are engaged in a range of services and activities to facilitate production, processing, and marketing of the cocoa. At a plant in La Paz, owned and managed by the federation, workers transform the raw organic cocoa into chocolate products. The cooperative industry employs about 100 men and women in various activities, from production to administration. Profits are returned to the native producers—a benefit seldom available to small farmers. As of 1994, El Ceibo's annual earnings from exports totalled $600,000 for cocoa beans and chocolate products. Chocolate consumers in the North can appreciate a product that is pesticide-free and also produced in a socially sound way.

El Ceibo was initially established in 1978 when a dozen small cooperatives of Aymara and Quechua immigrants settled and formed a federation along the Rio Beni. The co-op members had left the Andean highlands in the 1950s for this unfamiliar humid tropical territory, but maintained many of

nual exports of organic cacao beans and chocolate products are worth about $600,000.[293]

In El Salvador, small farmers in cooperatives have been relatively successful at NTAE production. A large project, coordinated by the Cooperative League of the U.S. (CLUSA) is providing marketing and technical support for about 45 cooperatives that produce some 39 million pounds of vegetables, flowers, and fruits for

---

Box 13. (continued)

their distinctive local traditions, particularly the Andean forms of collaboration and social organization. Drawing on traditional Aymara practices, the organization has an effective management system, frequently rotating leaders, ensuring equity of wages, and holding consensus-building assemblies. El Ceibo also sponsors cultural festivals that feature music and dances from the highlands. But El Ceibo also combines traditional practices with "modern" knowledge and techniques, providing training in business, finance, and agronomy, and sending some of its members to study in universities in La Paz and even abroad.

El Ceibo's chocolate is sold in various forms in domestic markets. The earnings are distributed equitably to the producer members through a well-monitored management system. Respect for reciprocal community obligations is a central value of the culture, and it helps to ensure sharing of the fruits of this business. This works: Making effective use of traditional approaches, El Ceibo has become one of the most widely known and respected cooperatives in Bolivia.

Source: Kevin Healy, "El Ceibo: Andean Traditional Organization and International Chocolate," *Culture and Development*, 1993 vol. 35, 1994; and personal communication, Kevin Healy, May 1994.

---

the U.S. and European markets each year.[294] Each coop has about 50 members, including both men and women. The project, supported by $9 million from USAID, involves the transfer of production technology, investment promotion and quality control, strengthening business management, training, and a "bottom-up" information management system. CLUSA plans to promote production of organic cashews in the future.[295]

Box 14. Organic Coffee Spreads the Benefits of Healthy Cultivation

Small-scale resource-poor farmers in Latin America are increasingly involved in producing gourmet organic coffee for export, meeting and stimulating a growing demand among Northern coffee connoisseurs. Organic coffee production has emerged partly in response to difficult economic conditions. During the late 1980s and early 1990s, the international market price for regular coffee declined dramatically to about US$0.70 per pound.

To surmount serious economic difficulties, alternative markets and new forms of organization, some small farmers began producing gourmet coffees to meet Northern consumers' growing demands. Gourmet coffee represents about 25 percent of the $5 billion coffee industry, and organic coffee constitutes about 1 percent of the gourmet coffee industry—approximately $12.5 million in market value worldwide. Although still a relatively small niche market, organic coffee is the fastest growing of the gourmet types. It has strong market potential in the future and sells for about twice as much as regular types, up to US$1.41 per pound (import prices) in European markets.

Organic coffee producers have formed effective organizations in the Caribbean and Latin America. An important producer organization is the Frente de Cafetaleros Solidarios de America Latina (The Consolidated Coffee Front in Latin America), which is co-evolving with the "Solidarity Market" in Europe and North America. This organization has 18 federations of cooperatives of indigenous communities from 10 countries. So far, 90 percent of the farmers in the group are from the Dominican Republic, Peru, Bolivia, Haiti, and Guatemala, but the organization is spreading to other countries. Like other similar producer associations, this group is showing that sustainable management and a community approach can help to build positive social and economic benefits of coffee production.

Box 14. (continued)

Another example of success in organic coffee production is Aztec Harvest, a coffee company owned collectively by five small farmer cooperatives in the three Mexican states of Chiapas, Oaxaca, and Guerrero. This company helps to eliminate dependence on middlemen, who often pay unfair prices. Nearly 1,000 farmers from 42 villages participate in Aztec, which will produce 5 million pounds of organic coffee in 1995. The co-ops are certified through the Organic Crop Improvement Association (OCIA) which inspects the farms regularly. Besides fetching high prices that benefit poor communities, organic coffee has agroecological advantages: the chemical-free soils on which it is grown are rich and healthy, many types of coffee plants are grown, the crop is planted among natural vegetation and shade trees, which helps to maintain biodiversity, prevent soil erosion, and reduce susceptibility to pests. Also worth noting, organic production methods resemble the indigenous methods used by many producers' parents before chemicals were widely adopted. Although labor costs are high where organic coffee is produced, the methods are efficient and profitable.

In mid-April of 1994, the First International Conference on Organic Coffee was held in Chiapas. Participants included more than 200 producers and technical advisors from farmer organizations throughout Mexico and Central America, as well as buyers from North America and Europe. This event illustrates the growing commitment and enthusiasm of the people involved, as well as the expanding spread of economic benefits from organic NTAE markets.

Sources: David Griswold, 1994, "In Harmony with the Rainforest," *Grassroots*, August/September, p. 27–29; and IFOAM, *Ecology and Farming*, Note on "Organic Coffee," from Food Matters Worldwide, July 1993; and L. von Foerster, personal communication, July 1994.

Another notable case is the rapid growth of organic coffee production in Latin America and the Caribbean. *(See Box 14.)* Although coffee has been a traditional export, organically-grown coffee is considered a non-traditional product since it requires distinct production methods and is grown for high-value specialty markets. The international price for organic coffee is twice that of regular coffee, and this new brew has become the fastest growing type of gourmet coffee in the United States and Europe.[296] Organic coffee is being produced by farmer associations such as cooperatives, which are becoming increasingly well-organized. These organizations can avoid intermediaries and sell directly to specialty businesses, enabling the producers to reap more of the benefits.

Some import entrepreneurs in the North have also developed initiatives to build the organic market and to improve the sustainability and equity of NTAEs. A particularly remarkable and original initiative is the "Seeds of Change" project, based in Santa Fe, New Mexico, which purchases organic seeds from smallholders in Latin America. *(See Box 15.)* In addition, a few non-government organizations in the North have also helped to build alternative markets for organic crops or for other exotic exports such as *tagua* (an ivory-like tree product being promoted by the U.S.-based environmental organization Conservation International).

Some caveats deserve mention in assessing the potential benefits of organic production, however. Although they are expanding, organic markets are still small niche markets and they can be difficult for producers to access. Also, organic production requires intimate knowledge of agroecological conditions, including the crops' and pests' natural enemies, soil qualities, nutrient cycling, and ways to manage these factors. In many cases, organic production requires specialized information. Indigenous populations tend to possess such knowledge of traditional crops, such as quinoa, cacao, and medicinal plants, but the diseases and pests of exotic crops like broccoli, snow peas, and strawberries require new information that can be difficult to obtain. Organic producers also need to link with specialized marketing agents, which is not easy in many cases. These factors are usually surmountable, but they demonstrate the importance of gaining access to adequate and appropriate information for production and marketing.

Box 15. Seeds of Change: An original initiative in organic NTAEs

Seeds of Change (SOC), an organic seed company based in Santa Fe, New Mexico, has undertaken an innovative import-export project to address many of the social and environmental problems sometimes associated with NTAEs. SOC currently purchases organic fruit, vegetable and flower seeds from growers in Costa Rica and Bolivia, which it then sells through catalogs in the United States and Canada. The organization also has similar programs in early stages of development in Mexico, El Salvador, Nicaragua, Guatemala, Honduras, and Belize.

Establishing contracts through existing NGOs and cooperatives, SOC works in partnership with producers to train personnel about organic farming (both on-site and in the United States), and to provide technical assistance on crop cultivation and on marketing of the product. SOC's overall goals are to preserve biodiversity and further sustainable agricultural development. It promotes the production of local seed varieties already familiar to smaller scale growers, and encourages diversity in producers' planting practices, both for agroecological benefits and to minimize economic dependence upon export seed crops.

SOC works with producers to ensure understanding of and compliance with complex import and export regulations, so all partners share responsibility in meeting these requirements. Ultimately, however, SOC attempts to pay as many of the transaction costs as possible. Producers are paid by SOC in U.S. currency through their local organizations, so that returns to the producers are maximized. The company is largely self-sufficient financially, though it relies on some outside funding for training and other services.

The Seeds of Change project in Latin America avoids many of the shortcomings of other NTAEs. First, organic crops require lower capital investment than other export crops, since pesticides frequently comprise a significant portion of total input costs. Second, because SOC works with groups of pro-

Box 15. (continued)

ducers, risks to individual growers are diminished. Third, SOC also offers a longer-term commitment to its producers than might commercial NTAE exporters, whose interests may change dramatically from one year to the next. Fourth, producers working with SOC are not dependent upon any single crop or source of income for their livelihoods, since their fields are diversified. Finally, the producer partnerships can help increase local incomes as well as protect the environment.

Seeds of Change's people-centered approach to business is unusual in the NTAE arena. On balance, it represents a socially conscious, ecologically sound alternative approach to NTAE development.

Source: Howard Shapiro, Seeds of Change, Vice President and Chief Agricultural Officer, personal communication June, 1994

D. Initiatives to Address Social Impacts: Organization and Grassroots Movements

Resource-poor farmers may be able to reap a greater share of the benefits of NTAEs if they are well-organized. Generally, with better organization comes greater social cohesion, community development, more group economic enterprises, and greater bargaining power. Conversely, some early NTAE cooperatives collapsed during the 1970s and early 1980s, mainly due to a lack of entrepreneurial experience. Yet, as noted earlier, experience in Guatemala, Bolivia, Mexico, and other countries show how well-organized farmers can market their produce more effectively.

In Ecuador, a newly formed association is helping smallholders produce mini-vegetables and broccoli. This project, supported by USAID and PROEXANT, has emerged partly as a response to political pressures to give attention to smallholders perspectives in NTAE schemes. CLUSA in El Salvador, is also working to strengthen organizational and business management capacity, as well as technical dimensions of cultivation. An African example comes from Ghana, where the Export Promotion Council is helping to build "Export Production Villages" that join together organizations of small resource-poor farmers to produce and market NTAEs. *(See Box 16.)* Lessons from such experiences could possibly be adapted and used in Latin America.

E. Challenges and Grassroots Reactions

Efforts to integrate social concerns into NTAE production work toward making agriculture development more sustainable and equitable. But such initiatives are few, tend to have internal weaknesses, such as lack of management experience and weak bargaining power, and are beset by external constraints that include a lack of financial support, credit and marketing services from governments, and inadequate access to markets, technology, and information. Often, the predominant economic policies and market competition are biased against small producer associations and alternative non-conventional strategies. Yet, if producer associations become funded and managed by state agencies or donors, they may lose control over their own activities or grow reliant on foreign funds that could be cut off unexpectedly.

Grassroots groups are rising to the challenge posed by these critical issues. Some farmer groups have demanded better access to opportunities through export marketing. But many *campesino* groups in Latin America have complained and sometimes denounced the export-oriented model of development and structural adjustment policies, mainly because such strategies have given insufficient attention to local food needs, access to credit, technologies, and marketing information. In the view of many of these farmers, the NTAE programs have left smallholders too vulnerable to price declines and have made it necessary to increase the use of expensive chemicals, as well as causing other problems. These farmers—notably those in Costa Rica and Guatemala—are holding demonstrations and large public meetings, lobbying for social

131

Box 16. Learning from Ghana's Export Production Villages

In Ghana, increasing numbers of smallholders are involved or interested in producing non-traditional agroexports. Yet, many of these rural producers have trouble linking into the export marketing networks. To better coordinate opportunities for these farmers, the Ghana Export Production Council (EPC) has initiated a unique program that organizes numerous smallholders into village companies owned and managed by producer shareholders. These companies, called Export Production Villages (EPVs) have been established in seven villages and three more are planned. Modelled partly after successful experiences in Sri Lanka, the EPV idea has been adapted to Ghanaian conditions. The objectives of the EPV program are to:

- develop an effective institutional mechanism for planning and coordinating rural based export production and marketing;
- create regulated and guaranteed markets for rural export production;
- ensure the availability of supplies for farmers, and link them to exporters;
- develop, improve, and sustain entrepreneurship, production efficiency and quality consciousness among rural producers;
- create or enhance employment and income opportunities in the rural area and improve producers' living standards.

Ghana's seven EPVs are located in three regions. Planned villages will produce and market yams, chili pepper and cashew nuts. These EPVs offer significant opportunities for small farmers, though the long-term effects have yet to be seen.

Source: Ghana Export Promotion Council, 1992, and Okyeame Ampadu-Agyei, Environmental Protection Council, 1994, preliminary report on NTAE policies.

change by the government, and suggesting alternatives to NTAE strategies. On several occasions, thousands of rural people have joined together to publicly voice their concerns and to propose reforms. In many cases, national NGOs have backed and coordinated these grassroots efforts, which has helped to strengthen their impact.

Among the groups working on such efforts in Costa Rica are Fondo de Desarrollo Agropecuario, Nuestra Tierra, Coordinadora de Organismos No Gubermentales con Proyectos Alternativos de Desarrollo, Centro de Capacitación para el Desarrollo (CECADE), Consejo Nacional de Justicia y Desarrollo.[297] All of these NGOs directly support the initiatives and interests of grassroots farmers and workers. They distribute publications, hold large formal policy dialogue, and organize demonstrations.

In Costa Rica, the Foro Emaus in Costa Rica is another remarkable alliance of about 25 grassroots organizations that has organized thousands of people in peaceful demonstrations to express concern and open policy dialogue about the expansion of agroexport production.[298] This large social movement focussed mainly on actions to stop the adverse socioeconomic and environmental impacts of banana companies; yet it urges changes in the general agroexport model, including the NTAE strategy and structural adjustment policies in general. In Guatemala, AVANCSO (Asociacion para el Avance de las Ciencias Sociales en Guatemala) and COINDE (Consejo de Instituciones de Desarrollo) are key organizations involved in gathering information and coordinating grassroots efforts concerned about the impacts of NTAE growth. They have also helped to convene local groups and draw attention to the interests of resource-poor farmers, largely indigenous peoples. Before the 1990s, many poor farmers in Guatemala were unable to engage in such organized efforts, due to serious repression and risk of political violence. Although such risks still exist, the campesino groups and NGOs have become increasingly capable in analysis and policy dialogues on these crucial issues.

What have such grassroots initiatives accomplished? So far, policy negotiations and other actions have helped raise awareness of the problems associated with export-oriented policies. In response, in a few cases, as in Costa Rica and Guatemala, some government officials and development agencies have reacted to *campesinos'* concerns and developed measures such as technical assistance or transport services for new commercial crops. Yet, the support of and responses to these grassroots interests are usually limited and need to be much greater. Incentives for improvement are enormous considering the high social and environmental costs of the present patterns of growth for the global supermarket.

VI.
DISCUSSION AND IMPLICATIONS

A. Persisting Dilemmas

Non-traditional agroexports in Latin America offer considerable benefits, opportunities, and financial promise, especially for capitalized investors who can survive market competition. Diversification of production in itself is promising. This recent boom has also generated jobs in developing countries and satisfies consumers in importing countries. But NTAEs' social costs, and risks, as well as environmental problems from heavy agrochemical use, cannot be ignored. While investments in NTAEs and other export sectors rise, resource deterioration continues, and hunger and insecurity among the majority of rural people grow. Although NTAE growth cannot be expected to solve all of Latin America's persistent rural development problems, some of the current patterns of growth in this sector repeat and reinforce the problems of past agroexport-led strategies. Countries involved in NTAE production sometimes with the assistance of development agencies such as USAID, are beginning to develop the capacities and programs to stave off or mitigate these adverse outcomes. But, innovative efforts to improve social and environmental conditions require much more support.

As the report has shown, economic production, ecological factors, and social conditions are inextricably interlinked; hence, trade-liberalization strategies, such as NAFTA and GATT, and export-led growth must be combined with policy measures to ensure sustainability. The proximate causes of environmental and socioeconomic problems in this sector, such as lack of information or capital and weak institutional capacities, must be overcome. But along with this, more fundamental features of NTAE production, such as

135

the emphasis on the short-term maximization of earnings (determined largely by market demands), development policies, and inequities in the distribution of resources in rural Latin America must also be addressed. These persisting dilemmas raise questions about the future: How can the benefits and opportunities of NTAE growth be spread more widely through institutional and policy changes? Can support for export growth be better balanced with policies to ensure that the majority of the rural poor have local food security? These questions remain critical policy challenges.

B. Developing a Framework for Change

Significant changes summarized below—ranging from broad agroexport policy reforms to consumers' and producers' behavioral changes—are needed in all sectors to confront the underlying roots of the socioeconomic and environmental problems associated with NTAEs and to expand alternative opportunities in this field. Policymakers, public institutions, non-government organizations (NGOs), and producers will need to reform agricultural development strategies. Groups in both the North and the South need to coordinate their efforts in undertaking such transformations.

To help identify priority problems and workable solutions, multisectoral workshops were held in 1993 in Ecuador and Guatemala as part of this project on NTAEs. The participants—a broad range of groups and individuals with experience in NTAEs and agricultural development issues—included representatives from smallholder farmer organizations, NGOs, farmworker groups, agribusinesses, agrochemical suppliers, research and educational institutions, government agencies, and development agencies (USAID and World Bank). After discussing research findings, problems, and promises, the workshop participants reached consensus on priority concerns about NTAEs and suggested actions and policies, as summarized in Appendix 4. These findings help define more sustainable agricultural policies for these particular countries, and illustrate concerns of local groups in Latin America. The process that led to them—discussions and negotiations among multiple interest groups—could be used in other countries where policy reforms are needed.

Based on suggestions emerging from such multisectoral workshops, along with analysis of empirical findings and key policy issues in this project, priority strategic principles and recommended policy reforms can be identified. These priorities can fit into an integrative framework of sustainable agriculture, oriented to promote economic productivity, environmental soundness, and social equity in rural development, as described in the beginning of this report. *(See Figure 3.)* The goals of social equity and sustainability are important in this context not only for ethical and welfare reasons, but also because they are necessary conditions for reaching broad economic goals. Moreover, as experience shows, exclusionary growth provokes social and political conflicts and exacerbates environmental degradation. More inclusive rural policies can play a critical role in development successes.[299]

C. Strategic Principles and Actions for Sustainable Agricultural Development

Within this general framework, *six strategic principles* are essential to develop policy changes and other actions affecting NTAEs and the broader strategies of agricultural development and trade. *(See Box 17.)*

Below, the priority responsibilities and actions of key interest groups are identified under each guiding principle.

1. Promote participatory approaches, especially by including poorer farmers and workers in agricultural development decision-making and in socioeconomic opportunities.

a. Policy Decision-makers (North and South)
Through multisectoral and participatory policy dialogue, various interest groups can participate in problem-solving, aimed at widening political perspectives, and building institutional capacities for cooperation and negotiation. This strategy is particularly vital to resolve environmental-economic conflicts among various groups.

If development agencies and national governments do not facilitate participatory decision-making in setting agricultural poli-

Box 17. A Summary of Strategic Principles to Guide Policies and Actions for Sustainable Agricultural Development

1. Promote participatory approaches, focussing on the inclusion of poor farmers and workers in agricultural development decision-making and in socioeconomic opportunities.

2. Build a policy environment to mitigate/avoid adverse impacts of NTAEs and to support and multiply sustainable and equitable patterns of trade and agricultural development;

3. Promote and develop sustainable agricultural technologies, stressing IPM, organic practices, and diversity, through changes by all actors in the production-market chain.

4. Build a better balance in policy attention to local vs. export production, placing priority on alleviating hunger and fulfilling local food security needs.

5. Increase the empowerment and status of poor producers and workers in production and marketing, to overcome market barriers and to promote equitable alternatives.

6. Increase information on the market conditions and impacts of agroexports, and improve access to such information to a wide audience of interested people.

cies, it is unlikely that broad-based sustainable development will be achieved. Currently, a narrow range of institutions and political leaders generally control NTAE decision-making, while representatives of environmental NGOs, public sector environmental agencies, workers' associations, smallholder farmers' associations, public health institutions, and agroecology groups have little or no influence. If national and international decision-makers involved a broader diversity of interests in both policy dialogue and decision-making on agricultural development, policies and programs would probably be more effective in generating lasting and equitable benefits. Setting up workshops among multiple interest groups, such as those mentioned above, is one way to initiate this process. Establishing public forums for debate and democratic elections on key development and trade issues are additional measures to build participatory approaches.

b. Producers, Consumers, Workers, and NGOs:
Other agricultural interest groups also need to mobilize themselves to make policy decision-making more inclusive. Farmers' organizations, marketing associations, workers, and consumers—especially those that are disadvantaged and usually excluded—need to negotiate with national agencies, pressuring for full participation in policy planning related to agricultural and trade policies such as NAFTA that affect them. The better organized these interest groups are, the greater their chances of success.

Workers and small producers—who are rarely consulted or involved in any kind of policy deliberations—especially need to work on such initiatives. Women as well as men must participate, given women's important roles in this agroexport sector. Consumer groups can also play a significant role in influencing public opinion, by using media reports or lobbying, for example, to pressure for change. In many cases, NGOs and policy research institutions can also help to facilitate and organize such participatory policy dialogue on agricultural development issues.

2. Build a policy environment to mitigate or avoid the adverse impacts of NTAEs and to support and multiply sustainable and equitable patterns of trade and agricultural development.

a. Policy Decision-makers at the National Level
While some policies increasingly favor export expansion, development agencies and governments must launch other policy and institutional changes in both the North and South to help minimize the adverse social impacts of agroexports, support local food needs, and make agriculture more sustainable. Six policy reforms by governments are particularly urgent:

Environmental sustainability policy reforms

(i) Better enforce pesticide policies to avoid negative impacts of pesticides, by: strengthening controls of toxic products to protect farmworkers' health; strengthening inspections and enforcement measures to reduce pesticide-residue accumulation in local foods and the environment, as well as exported foods; and providing full information and education on all pesticide products, instructions for use, risks, and precautions;

(ii) remove policy incentives (such as subsidies, tax discounts, and credit obligations) for using high inputs of pesticides;

(iii) carry out rigorous environmental impact reviews of agro-export programs, and implement policy measures in trade agreements to avoid potential adverse impacts of expanding trade.

Socioeconomic policy issues

(iv) provide equitable access to credit and marketing services to farmers, especially to smallholders in associations, for improving production and marketing;

(v) provide technical assistance and information to producers (especially smallholders) on diverse NTAEs and production options, quality standards, and market prices;

(vi) establish provisions in trade and marketing policies to ensure that benefits of trade expansion are spread to the needy and that labor rights are protected.

Determining the specific policy changes needed in each country requires analyzing local needs and making adjustments for specific conditions. To implement such policies, ministries of agriculture, labor, and health must coordinate their activities and develop effective implementation capacities.

b. Development Agencies and Northern Policy-makers
Policy-makers and development agencies in the United States and other NTAE-importing countries must support broad policy changes that help build sustainability and equity of NTAEs. Four priorities stand out:

(i)   incorporate and implement environmental and social provisions in trade agreements such as NAFTA and encourage governments to develop such policies, to mitigate adverse effects of NTAE expansion and promote sustainable growth;

(ii) establish and spread information (to governments, producers, and exporters) on consistent standards for residue tolerances, phytosanitary rules, and organic markets;

(iii) establish and implement rigorous guidelines for conducting environmental impact reviews of NTAE activities;

(iv) relax aesthetic standards on imported produce to reduce pressures on farmers to apply chemicals heavily.

c. Agrochemical Input Companies
These actors must comply with both existing and new policies and regulations affecting agrochemical inputs, especially those dealing with safety guidelines and information diffusion on characteristics of pesticides. They must also fully disclose information and participate in policy discussions to help decision-makers establish appropriate policies on pesticides. Such practices can pay off for businesses, especially in the long run.

3. Promote and develop sustainable agricultural technologies and practices, stressing IPM, organic practices, and crop diversity, through changes by all actors.

A technological transformation to sustainable agricultural practices is imperative. Such changes are not easy, and many groups must work together to develop and implement new practices. Though precedents exist, much more work is needed on the following key points to build up and spread effective and sustainable technical alternatives:

a. National and International Decision-makers
In both national and international agencies, key steps are to:

(i)   support technical assistance (e.g., extension services) and training on the diffusion and adoption of Integrated Pest Management (IPM) practices;

141

(ii) develop and support programs for diffusion of information, as well as training courses on organic production, taking advantage of expanding new market opportunities;
(iii) support training and technical assistance programs on agroecological practices, particularly stressing the value of diversified farming systems, and crops adapted to local environmental conditions and to farmers' capacities.

b. Producers

Since farmers need to be key actors in the implementation of sustainable agricultural technologies, three changes in practice are vital:

(i) implement Integrated Pest Management practices, which help minimize pesticide costs and control pests effectively;
(ii) adopt organic production methods, especially where there are market opportunities;
(iii) incorporate agroecological principles into farming practices;
(iv) participate in training courses on IPM, organic methods, and other agroecological practices.

c. Agrochemical Input Suppliers and Marketers

Other agribusinesses, particularly companies that sell and distribute pesticides and other agrochemical inputs also have responsibilities to change certain practices that have provoked problems. Most immediately, they should:

(i) strictly adhere to international standards and codes and national laws that regulate the marketing of toxic substances, focussing on minimizing risks to users and local populations, and providing complete information on products they sell;
(ii) stop using commission sales systems (which leads to overprescribing and contributes to the overuse of chemicals) for pesticides;
(iii) become better educated about IPM and work with other groups to support alternatives.

Such changes are urgently needed for ethical reasons; and for some companies they may initially translate into sales reductions.

But for most companies, and society more generally, benefits will follow reforms, especially in the long run. The measures can pay off and even improve business over time and self-defeating patterns of pesticide use can be avoided. In addition, consumer satisfaction and safety can be improved, the costs of pest resistance and residue violations can be reduced, and production can be made more sustainable.

At the same time, export firms and brokers that market export products have to take responsibility to:

(i)   promote a reduction in the use of pesticides, especially to comply with residue regulations;

(ii) encourage the use of other sustainable production technologies, providing technical assistance and training;

(iii) promote diversity of crops/varieties, providing information to producers on crops with market potential.

c. Consumers and NGOs:

Consumer groups and other NGOs—especially those in the North—need to:

(i)   educate the public on the adverse effects of demand for "blemish-free" produce, and encourage consumers and food distributors to relax high aesthetic standards.

(ii) advocate reliable certification for IPM or organically grown produce;

(iii) purchase only those imported products that have been organically grown or used sustainable technologies, whenever possible.

4. Balance policy attention toward local vs. export production, placing priority on alleviating hunger and fulfilling local food security needs.

a. Policy Decision-makers (international and national)

Policy support is needed for the local production of basic food supplies, to ensure food security and to complement current support for exports. International development agencies and donors in the North, along with governments in the Latin American region need to give priority attention to hunger alleviation. Although this study has shown that, in some cases, export strategies can help contribute to increased incomes for the poor, hunger is still widespread. Therefore, technical support programs and agricultural policies must be revised to ensure credit, technologies, and fair prices for locally-marketed crops, to improve the wellbeing of the poor.

b. Producers

Producers need to respond to the need to feed local populations, as well as to invest in export-oriented production. Logically, they will react to market opportunities and price signals—whether for local or export markets—which are influenced by the policies mentioned above. But, independently, they can also gain by balancing production strategies and avoiding dependency on exports alone. Generally, farmers can spread their risks by also planting crops for local markets. Moreover, producers' increased investments in local production can help demonstrate to decision-makers the need for policy attention to food security.

c. NGOs and Consumers

Nongovernmental groups interested in agricultural development, in both the North and the South, also need to do more to encourage decision-makers to pay closer attention to food security priorities and to alleviate local hunger, thus counterbalancing the attention to exports. They should disseminate information on the impacts of exports and local food needs, lobby for policy changes, and carry out applied research on such issues. Consumer groups must call attention to these needs as well.

5. Help empower and increase the status of poor producers and workers in production and marketing to overcome barriers and to promote equitable opportunities.

Direct action and participation of farmers, workers, and other community groups are crucial in developing sustainable agricultural practices. As made clear here, actions by these groups are emerging throughout Latin America. With strong potential capabilities and urgent needs, they must become empowered by gaining policy-makers' attention, becoming more involved in decision-making, and implementing changes—thus increasing their political and socioeconomic status.

a. Policy Decision-makers

Reforms and programs by governments and development agencies are needed to encourage the participation of grassroots groups and farmer associations, and to promote opportunities for empowerment of disadvantaged agricultural producers and workers. Although some efforts have been initiated by USAID and other groups, more work is needed to:

(i)   provide support and focus public attention on existing initiatives and interests to develop opportunities for poor farmers and workers in commercial agriculture, particularly women;

(ii) protect fair pricing (through legal means) and defend fair terms and enforcement of contracts for producers, especially those who are vulnerable to unfair pricing by buyers;

(iii) enforce labor laws and worker health protection for those involved in NTAE production and ensure that workers earn fair wages.

(iv) protect rights and encourage opportunities for women to benefit more fairly in NTAEs, not only in wage labor, but also in ownership of farms or businesses; and

(v)   support the formation of organizations among smallholders producing NTAEs and encourage the removal of impediments (such as membership fees to trade organizations) to their involvement.

b. Producers

Smallholder producers also need to work to overcome marketing impediments in the production-market chain, and to gain opportunities. Strategic actions include:

(i)   form producer associations (e.g., cooperatives) that can help increase access to markets and information, and strengthen production capacities;

(ii) develop direct market contracts with importers to gain needed price information, to obtain higher prices for produce, and to avoid dependency on intermediaries for marketing; and

(iii) encourage production diversity to spread risks and improve competitive positions.

c. Workers' Actions and Rights

Workers in this sector also need to work together to assert their rights in agroexport businesses. Priority actions include:

(i) ensure that all laborers have full information on their legal rights and work to gain enforcement of those rights;

(ii) organize to protect workers' health, especially vis-a-vis pesticides, and work with managers and policy-makers to gain adequate protective gear and health services;

(iii) form worker associations to help improve negotiation and bargaining capacities, especially to gain contracts and rights.

d. Consumers and NGOs

Consumers and NGOs in the North who purchase crops imported from the tropics can also make changes in behavior that could help address NTAE problems. They need to:

(i) choose sustainably grown (such as organic) products, especially by smallholder associations, whenever possible; and

(ii) help raise awareness among the public and policy-makers of the need for sustainable equitable approaches to agricultural production that benefit the poor and protect health.

6. Increase information on market conditions and impacts of agroexports, and improve access to such information to a broad audience of interested people.

Gaps remain in the understanding of market conditions, the impacts, and the potential of NTAEs. As production grows, more data on NTAEs must be gathered and access to such information must be improved, especially for disadvantaged farmers and small entrepreneurs who lack data that is vital for their survival in the business. Researchers institutes and scientists, NGOs, and government agencies, have responsibilities to help fill these gaps. Research priorities include the impacts of pesticides and the use of Integrated Pest Management for NTAE production; local and export markets for organic markets; worker health risks, especially for women, in NTAE production and processing; and the distribution of economic benefits in this sector. This may require improved systems for monitoring the results of agroexport growth.

The above principles and recommended actions are both ambitious and difficult to implement, but they are attainable through commitment and hard work by many actors together. More fundamental changes in political regimes may be needed to address the root causes of persisting hunger and rural environmental degradation in the rural sector. In particular, overcoming the inequities in Latin America's agricultural sector is often seen as a necessary cornerstone for a truly meaningful transformation in development patterns. But, even if such profound reforms cannot be made, carrying out the strategic principles and actions outlined above will help avoid the "bitter" traits of agroexport growth, and work towards feasible reforms and beneficial alternatives.

Integrating environmental sustainability and equity concerns into agriculture is crucial to the viability and success of any development strategy. Opportunities are increasing for the growth of NTAE markets in the global economy, especially as international trade agreements are being strengthened; so measures taken now to ensure that trade relations are sustained and equitable can have substantial positive impacts. Policies and actions such as those identified here may help other countries avoid troubles in the NTAE sector and reap harvests that have lasting social and economic benefits.

Lori Ann Thrupp is a senior associate and Director of Sustainable Agriculture in the World Resources Institute's Center for International Development and Environment, where she works on agriculture and natural resources projects. Previously, she was a postdoctoral fellow at the University of California Berkeley, and also worked for two years on environmental policies, agroecology, and sustainable development in Costa Rica.

Gilles Bergeron is a Rockefeller postdoctoral research fellow working with the International Food Policy Research Institute on a hillside-agriculture research project in Central America. He previously worked as an associate at the Instituto de Nutrición de Centroamerica y Panama (INCAP), in Guatemala.

William F. Waters is a senior associate at the Center for International Health in George Washington University. Previously, he worked in Ecuador as Dean of Social Sciences and Humanities and, for a decade, as a professor of Sociology at the Universidad San Francisco de Quito.

APPENDICES

Appendix 1: List of Acronyms

APHIS	Animal and Plant Health Inspection Service
ARF	Agricultural Research Fund
ATPA	Andean Trade Preference Act
AVANCSO	Asociación Para el Avance de las Ciencias Sociales en Guatemala (Association for the Advancement of Social Sciences in Guatemala)
CAT	Certificado de Abono Tributario (Tributary Bond Certificate)
CATIE	Centro Agrícola Tropical de Investigación y Enseñanza (Agricultural Center for Tropical Research & Training)
CBI	Caribbean Basin Initiative
CDC	Commonwealth Development Corporation
CECADE	Centro de Capacitación para el Desarrollo (Center for Training and Development)
CEMAT	Centro Mesoamericano de Estudios Sobre Tecnología Apropiada (Mesoamerican Center for Studies on Appropriate Technology)
CFN	Corporación Financiar (National Finance Corporation)

CINDE	Costa Rica Investment and Development
CLUSA	Cooperative League of the United States
EPV	Export Production Villages
EXPOFLORES	Gremial de Exportadores de Flores (Ecuador) (Flower Growers Guild)
FEDEXPOR	Federación de Exportadores de Ecuador (Federation of Exporters)
FOB	Free on board
FUSADES	Foundation for Salvadorean Development
GATT	General Agreement on Tariffs and Trade
GEPC	Ghana Export Promotion Council
GEXPRONT	Gremial de Exportadores de Productos Notradicionales (Guatemalan Non-traditional Products Exporters' Association)
GIFAP	Groupement Internacional (International Group of National Associations of Agricultural Manufacturers)
GSP	General System of Preferences
ICTA	Instituto de Ciencia y Tecnología Agrícola (Institute of Agricultural Science and Technology)
IDB	Inter-American Development Bank
INCAP	Instituto de Nutrición de Centroamerica y Panama
IPM	Integrated Pest Management
ISI	Import Substitution Industrialization
NAFTA	North American Free Trade Agreement
NTAEs	Non-Traditional Agricultural Exports
OIA	Organic Crop Improvement Association
PDA	Agricultural Development Project
PIPPA	Programa Integral para Agricultura y Protección Ambiental (Integral Program for Agricultural & Environmental Protection)

PRODIVERSA Proyecto para la Diversificación Agricola (Project for Agricultural Diversification)

PROEXANT Programa para la Exportación Agricola Notradicional (Program for the Export of Non-traditional Agriculture)

ROCAP Regional Office of Central American Programs of USAID

SOC Seeds of Change

TNCs Transnational corporations

USAID United States Agency for International Development

USDA United States Department of Agriculture

USEPA United States Environmental Protection Agency

USFDA United States Food and Drug Administration

USFQ Universidad San Francisco de Quito (Ecuador)

WRI World Resources Institute

Appendix 2: Methodology for the Project

This study entailed the following activities and methods:

General Research:
1. Review and analysis of secondary data and literature on NTAEs in Latin America;
2. Interviews with policy decision-makers in the World Bank, USAID, and the Inter-American Development Bank.
3. Analysis of original data on pesticide residues from the U.S. Food and Drug Administration (obtained through the Freedom of Information Act)
4. Interviews with representatives of the private sector offices of USAID and NGOs in Costa Rica

Field research and collaborative activities in Ecuador:
1. Field survey of 105 workers and 54 technical managers in NTAE plantations in the highland region of Ecuador, focussing on pesticide-use issues and environmental questions;
2. A field survey of the majority of Ecuador's fresh flower producers on general production issues (William Waters, 1992);
3. Systematic interviews with policy officials and analysts who are concerned with NTAEs;
4. Analysis of primary production data;
5. Multi-institutional workshops (in Quito and Guyaquil) in June l992, to identify priority problems and opportunities of NTAEs;
6. A survey of 120 women workers on NTAE plantations and processing plants.

Field research and collaborative activities in Guatemala:
1. Review of secondary data;
2. Interviews with policy decision-makers, USAID representatives, researchers, and others involved in agricultural development;
3. Co-organization and co-facilitation of a multi-sectoral workshop on sustainability of non-traditional agroexports, held in October, 1993, which identified priority problems and opportunities, and policy implications on NTAEs (*see* proceedings: INCAP/WRI, 1994);
4. Informal survey and participatory workshops among women in Sacatapequez, Guatemala, on their involvement in NTAE production, benefits/costs, and perceptions of needed changes;
5. Field survey of producers and technical personnel regarding their perceptions and uses of Integrated Pest Management, the adoption rates, and benefits and costs of introducing such methods.

Details on the survey instruments and/or methodologies can be obtained upon request from World Resources Institute.

Appendix 3: U.S. FDA Detentions for Pesticide Residues in Shipments of Fruits and Vegetables Imported from Latin America, FY 1984–94

Total number of detentions[a]
(total estimate US$ value of shipments detained)[b]

	1984	1985	1986	1987
Chile	1 ($34,000)	1 ($1,000)	250 ($6,283,000)	5 ($82,000)
Colombia	0 ($0)	0 ($0)	0 ($0)	0 ($0)
Costa Rica	0 ($0)	1 ($0)	1 ($8,000)	2 ($9,000)
Dominican Republic	16 ($5,000)	6 ($25,000)	5 ($1,000)	39 ($13,000)
Ecuador	0 ($0)	0 ($0)	1 ($1,000)	0 ($0)
El Salvador	0 ($0)	0 ($0)	0 ($0)	0 ($0)
Guatemala	0 ($0)	10 ($5,000)	0 ($0)	3 ($11,000)
Honduras	0 ($0)	1 ($110,000)	0 ($0)	0 ($0)
Jamaica	1 ($4,000)	0 ($0)	2 ($4,000)	3 ($5,000)
Mexico	202 ($429,000)	1,196 ($15,397,000)	1,402 ($4,821,000)	1,351 ($4,711,000)

Appendix 3: (continued)

	1988	1989	1990	1991
Chile	13	178	17	19
	($266,000)	($1,211,000)	($751,000)	($164,000)
Colombia	3	2	1	7
	($17,000)	($1,000)	($0)	($15,000)
Costa Rica	6	17	28	9
	($52,000)	($50,000)	($35,000)	($26,000)
Dominican Republic	172	1350	254	173
	($114,000)	($10,563,000)	($233,000)	($185,000)
Ecuador	1	3	3	0
	($0)	($26,000)	($2,000)	($0)
El Salvador	3	1	0	14
	($469,000)	($3,000)	($0)	($215,000)
Guatemala	20	54	119	25
	($69,000)	($201,000)	($825,000)	($179,000)
Honduras	2	6	0	7
	($10,000)	($31,000)	($0)	($58,000)
Jamaica	13	14	6	18
	($16,000)	($12,000)	($4,000)	($17,000)
Mexico	1,462	425	369	192
	($22,362,000)	($960,000)	($1,097,000)	($1,242,000)

Source: WRI analysis of U.S. Food and Drug Administration data.

Notes: $0 = zero or less than $500.

a. Shipments are detained for pesticide testing when a random sampling of a small portion of a shipment indicates potential violations of FDA regulations, or when a product from a certain country is under automatic or common problematic detention, as is currently the case with snow peas from Guatemala and

1992	1993	1994[c]	Commonly Detained Products[d] (Common Problem Pesticides)
6 ($30,000)	23 ($164,000)	153 ($489,000)	grapes, berries (permethrins)
19 ($15,000)	30 ($118,000)	17 ($34,000)	berries, naranjilla (chlorothalanil, methamidaphos)
24 ($53,000)	7 ($78,000)	7 ($100,000)	berries, chayote (chlorothalanil, methamidaphos)
111 ($60,000)	85 ($36,000)	48 ($22,000)	long beans, eggplant, peppers (monocrotophos, methamidaphos)
3 ($112,000)	24 ($17,000)	0 ($0)	strawberries, cantaloupe (chlorothalanil)
20 ($288,000)	1 ($2,000)	0 ($0)	okra (methamidaphos)
569 ($2,074,000)	1,755 ($10,400,000)	613 ($4,208,000)	snow peas, broccoli (chlorothalanil, methamidaphos)
10 ($10,000)	40 ($50,000)	0 ($0)	snow peas, okra (chlorothalanil, methamidaphos)
21 ($32,000)	67 ($476,000)	5 ($13,000)	peppers, papaya (monocrotophos, kelthane)
309 ($1,687,000)	342 ($1,214,000)	179 ($669,000)	peppers, strawberries, mangos (methamidaphos)

a handful of products from the Dominican Republic. Many detained shipments are released for entry into the U.S. following testing.
b. Values are not exact due to possible minor inconsistencies or errors in measurement and calculation.
c. FY 1994 includes data through February 1994.
d. This list contains only some of the more common problematic products and pesticides, though in most cases many more were involved.

Appendix 4: Specific Recommended Actions and Policies Based on Multisectoral Workshops in Guatemala and Ecuador

A. Results from Guatemala

SOCIAL ASPECTS

Problems

Lack of organization among NTAE small farmers
Lack of training for farmers
Lack of food security for NTAE small farmers
Insufficient consideration of risks
Insufficient credit and extension services in NTAEs
Adverse effects on cultural conditions:
    heavy labor burden for women and children;
    losses in community and family activities;
    loss of communal solidarity;
Limitations in access to information, communication.

Recommended Actions/Policies

Form blocks or organizations of NTAE producers
Create systematic training programs in NTAEs
Strengthen programs for food security and nutrition
Include risks and adverse effects in accounting
Improve state support for credit for small farmers
Improve communication in NTAE programs
Maintain cultural identify through community action

Appendix 4. (continued)

Seek ways to alleviate heavy female/child labor
Promote farmer organization
Improve diffusion of information, especially through local promoters

ECONOMIC ASPECTS

Problems
Lack of information on prices for NTAEs
Lack of policies and strategies on prices, credit, market
Lack of political will to support small farmers in NTAEs
Lack of "entrepreneurial" orientation
Lack of intermediary channels (for markets)
Pressures of international & national competition (exchange rate, subsidies, technology)
Price fluctuations and low prices set by intermediaries for farmers

Recommended Actions/Policies
Gain access to information networks
Develop policies to meet rural needs (prices, credit)
Facilitate access to markets
Improve coordination between private actors
Process native products for export markets
Ensure that agroexport companies give fair values and opportunities to small farmers
Strengthen small farmers via strong associations
Improve economic and technical management in NTAEs
Form direct contracts with exporters/buyers

ECOLOGICAL ASPECTS

Problems
Contamination of flora, fauna, water, people, by chemicals
Inappropriate use and management of pesticides
Undervaluation of traditional customs that respect nature
Unethical behavior by producers and salespeople
Lack of institutions, laws, and policies on ecologically sustainable development and on organic agriculture

Lack of awareness of ecological sustainability
Excessive promotion of chemical inputs
Lack of implementation of laws and regulations
Lack of information on residues and their effects
Lack of awareness by intermediaries

Recommended Actions/Policies
Promote participation of civil society in conservation
Improve training/awareness on pesticides and alternatives
Develop research programs on the Mayan culture and its value for
    agricultural development
Create commissions on organic agriculture
Develop integrated and systematic training programs
Undertake more research/education on environmental issues
Maintain safety/health of workers and consumers
Apply laws, both by producers and state agencies
Improve research and residue monitoring capacities
Make intermediaries more aware of pesticide problems

Source: Adapted from multisectoral workshop co-sponsored by
INCAP and WRI in Antigua Guatemala, October 1993. See also
*Proceedings—Sostenibilidad de las Exportaciones Agricolas Notradi-
cionales para Pequeños Productores en Guatemala.* Instituto de Nutrición de Centroamerica y Panama. (Also, some information from
workshop on pesticides in snow peas with smallholders in December, 1993.)

Appendix 4. (continued)

B. Summary of Results in Ecuador

SOCIAL ASPECTS

Problems
Poor labor conditions, especially for women
Lack of application of labor laws
Lack of farmer education
Lack of services/support to small farmers
Lack of knowledge on pesticide risks and safety measures
Lack of information on occupational health
Constraint on workers' organizations

Strategies/Recommendations
Improve labor conditions, especially for women
Apply labor laws seriously
Launch education campaigns for farmers
Strengthen marketing associations
Increase training on pesticides and health protection
Prevent discriminatory labor practices
Raise awareness of workers about labor rights
Develop worker organizations to address concerns
Study gender issues in NTAEs

ECONOMIC ASPECTS

Problems
Lack of technology and information
Difficulties meeting market standards
Lack of market information/links
Lack of support by the state and donors

Strategies/Recommendations
Improve access to technology and information
Improve quality-control systems
Change policies to improve market opportunities: (e.g.)

Improve credit and insurance;
Offer economic incentives for export markets;
Develop training on marketing;
Create funds for the Ministry of Agriculture on NTAE services;
Promote trade associations.

ENVIRONMENTAL ASPECTS
Problems
Degradation of health and resources, mainly from improper use of
    pesticides
Lack of knowledge on pesticides and their alternatives
Irresponsibility of pesticide salesmen
Lack of crop diversity and rotation

Strategies/Recommendations
Apply pesticide laws and improve states' capacities to apply them
Improve pesticide residue monitoring
Encourage agrochemical companies to comply with laws and dis-
    close full information
Train all managers, policy-makers, salesmen, and workers in pesti-
    cide issues
Monitor worker health
Promote Integrated Pest Management
Institute crop rotation and diversification
Promote organic production where possible

Source: From multisectoral workshop cosponsored by USFQ, WRI,
and IICA in Quito and Guayaquil. June, 1992. *See also* proceedings:
Waters, W. (ed) Desafios en la Agroexportación Notraditional, Quito,
Ecuador, Universidad San Francisco de Quito, y World Resources
Institute. 1993. (With information from follow-up workshops held
in Ecuador in February 1994.)

NOTES

1. Alain de Janvry, *The Agrarian Question and Reformism in Latin America* (Baltimore, Md.: Johns Hopkins University Press, 1981); Victor Bulmer-Thomas, *The Political Economy of Central America Since 1920* (New York, N.Y.: Cambridge University Press, 1987).
2. Robert Williams, *Export Agriculture and the Crisis in Central America* (Chapel Hill, N.C.: University of North Carolina Press, 1986); Eva Paus, ed., *Struggle Against Dependence: Nontraditional Export Growth in Central America and the Caribbean* (Boulder, Colo.: Westview Press, 1988); D. Goodman and M. Redclift, "The Machinery of Hunger: the Crisis of Latin American Food Systems," in *Environment and Development in Latin America: The Politics of Sustainability* (Manchester: Manchester University Press, 1992).
3. For discussion of these findings and other debates about the impacts of agroexport production, see for examples: Simon Maxwell and Adrian Fernando, "Cash Crops in Developing Countries: The Issues, the Facts, the Policies," *World Development*, 1989, vol. 17, no. 11:1677–1989; Nigel Twose, *Cultivating Hunger: An Oxfam Study of Food, Power, and Poverty* (Oxford: Oxfam, 1984); A. de Janvry, *The Agrarian Question and Reformism in Latin America* (Baltimore, Md.: Johns Hopkins University Press, 1981); World Bank, *World Development Report* (Washington, D.C.: World Bank, 1986); Frances Moore Lappé and Joseph Collins, *Food First* (San Francisco, Calif.: Institute for Food and Development Policy, 1977).

4. United Nations Conference on Trade and Development (UNC-TAD), *Handbook of International Trade and Development Statistics* (Geneva: UNCTAD, 1991), Table 4.3; cited in Steven Jaffee, *Exporting High-Value Food Commodities: Success Stories from Developing Countries*, World Bank Discussion Papers number 198 (Washington, D.C.: World Bank, 1993).

5. United Nations Conference on Trade and Development (UNC-TAD), *Handbook of International Trade and Development Statistics* (Geneva: UNCTAD, 1991), Table 4.3; cited in Steven Jaffee, *Exporting High-Value Food Commodities: Success Stories from Developing Countries*, World Bank Discussion Papers number 198 (Washington, D.C.: World Bank, 1993).

6. U.S. Agency for International Development (USAID), Latin America and Caribbean Bureau, *Latin America and Caribbean Selected Economic and Social Data* (Washington, D.C.: USAID, 1993).

7. Cited in Michael Carter, Bradford Barham, Dina Mesbah, and Denise Stanley, "Agroexports and the Rural Resource Poor in Latin America: Policy Options for Achieving Broadly-Based Growth," unpublished draft paper, University of Wisconsin, Land Tenure Center, Madison, Wis., 1993; based on U.S. Department of Agriculture statistics.

8. From William F. Waters, based on statistics from Proyecto para Exportación Agrícola No-Tradicional (PROEXANT), *Informe Annual* (Quito, Ecuador: PROEXANT, 1992).

9. Steven Jaffee, *Exporting High-Value Food Commodities: Success Stories from Developing Countries*, World Bank Discussion Paper number 198 (Washington, D.C.: World Bank, 1993).

10. U.S. Food and Drug Administration, 1994; primary data analyzed by World Resources Institute.

11. *See* Chapter 4 of this report for details and citations on labor conditions.

12. Adapted from World Commission on Environment and Development, *Our Common Future* (New York, N.Y.: Oxford University Press, 1987).

13. Alain deJanvry, The Agrarian Question and Reformism in Latin America (Baltimore, Md.: Johns Hopkins University Press, 1981).

14. SIECA, VIII Compendio Estadístico para Centroamérica, 1978; cited in Tom Barry, *Roots of Rebellion: Land and Hunger in Central America* (Boston, Mass.: South End Press, 1987), 8. Recent census data are not available in the region.

15. David Goodman and Michael Redclift, "The Machinery of Hunger: the Crisis of Latin American Food Systems," in *Environment and Development in Latin America: The Politics of Sustainability* (Manchester: Manchester University Press, 1991).

16. Eva Paus, "Economic Development in Central America and the Caribbean: Role of Nontraditional Export Crops," in Eva Paus, ed., *Struggle Against Dependence: Nontraditional Export Growth in Central America and the Caribbean* (Boulder, Colo.: Westview Press, 1988), 2.

17. Jen-Paul Sajhau and Jürgen von Muralt, *Plantations and Plantation Workers* (Geneva: International Labour Organization of the United Nations, 1987).

18. Eva Paus, "Economic Development in Central America and the Caribbean: The Role of Nontraditional Exports," in Eva Paus, ed., *Struggle Against Dependence: Nontraditional Export Growth in Central America and the Caribbean* (Boulder, Colo.: Westview Press, 1988), 1; Morris Whitaker and D. Greene, "Development Policy and Agriculture," in M. Whitaker and D. Colyer, eds., *Agriculture and Economic Survival* (Boulder, Colo.: Westview Press, 1990), 23.

19. Robert Williams, *Export Agriculture and the Crisis in Central America* (Durham, N.C.: University of North Carolina, 1986).

20. Simon Maxwell and Adrian Fernando, "Cash Crops in Developing Countries: The Issues, the Facts, the Policies," *World Development*, 1989, vol. 17, no. 11:1679.

21. Victor Bulmer-Thomas, *The Political Economy of Central America Since 1920* (New York, N.Y.: Cambridge University Press, 1987); Simon Maxwell and Adrian Fernando, "Cash Crops in Developing Countries: The Issues, the Facts, the Policies," *World Development*, 1989, vol. 17, no. 11:1677–1708.

22. Bradford Barham, M. Carter, and W. Sigelko, *Adoption and Accumulation Patterns in Guatemala's Latest Agro-export Boom* (Madison, Wis.: University of Wisconsin, Social Systems Research Institute, 1992), 2.

23. Simon Maxwell and Adrian Fernando, "Cash Crops in Developing Countries: The Issues, the Facts, the Policies," *World Development,* 1989, vol. 17, no. 11:1679. See also Frances Moore Lappé and Joseph Collins, *World Hunger: Twelve Myths* (New York, N.Y.: Grove Press, 1986).

24. *See also* Frances Moore Lappé and Joseph Collins, *World Hunger: Twelve Myths* (New York, N.Y.: Grove Press, 1986); Nigel Twose, *Cultivating Hunger: An Oxfam Study of Food, Power, and Poverty* (Oxford: Oxfam Press, 1984); also *see* discussion in Simon Maxwell and Adrian Fernando, "Cash Crops in Developing Countries: The Issues, the Facts, the Policies," *World Development,* 1989, vol. 17, no. 11:1679.

25. Robert Williams, *Export Agriculture and the Crisis in Central America* (Chapel Hill, N.C.: University of North Carolina Press, 1986); Eva Paus, ed., *Struggle Against Dependence: Nontraditional Export Growth in Central America and the Caribbean* (Boulder, Colo.: Westview Press, 1988); D. Goodman and M. Redclift, "The Machinery of Hunger: the Crisis of Latin American Food Systems," in *Environment and Development in Latin America: The Politics of Sustainability* (Manchester: Manchester University Press, 1992).

26. Robert Williams, *Export Agriculture and the Crisis in Central America* (Chapel Hill, N.C.: University of North Carolina Press, 1986); Eva Paus, ed., *Struggle Against Dependence: Nontraditional Export Growth in Central America and the Caribbean* (Boulder, Colo.: Westview Press, 1988); D. Goodman and M. Redclift, "The Machinery of Hunger: the Crisis of Latin American Food Systems," in *Environment and Development in Latin America: The Politics of Sustainability* (Manchester: Manchester University Press, 1992).

27. Robert Williams, *Export Agriculture and the Crisis in Central America* (Chapel Hill, N.C.: University of North Carolina Press, 1986); L.A. Thrupp, "The Political Ecology of Sustainable Rural Development: Dynamics of Social and Natural Resource Degradation," in *Food for the Future: Conditions and Contradictions of Sustainability* (New York, N.Y.: John Wiley and Sons, 1992). For more details on these effects, see also L.A. Thrupp, "Persistent Environmental and Equity Dilemmas in Latin

America's Agroexport Booms," in *The Politics of Latin American Environmental Policy* (San Diego, Calif.: University of California, forthcoming in 1995).

28. World Bank cited in Reed Hertford, "Towards a Strategy for Investment in the Agricultural Research System of the Americas," draft paper, Inter-American Development Bank, Washington, D.C., 1994, p. 4.

29. World Bank cited in Reed Hertford, "Towards a Strategy for Investment in the Agricultural Research System of the Americas," draft paper, Inter-American Development Bank, Washington, D.C., 1994, p. 4.

30. Latin American and Caribbean Commission on Development and Environment, *Our Own Agenda* (Washington, D.C.: Inter-American Development Bank and United Nations Development Programme, 1992), 19.

31. Latin American and Caribbean Commission on Development and Environment, *Our Own Agenda* (Washington, D.C.: Inter-American Development Bank and United Nations Development Programme, 1992), 19.

32. Douglas Southgate, "Development of Ecuador's Renewable Natural Resources" in M. Whitaker and D. Colyer, eds., *Agriculture and Economic Survival* (Boulder, Colo.: Westview Press, 1990).

33. Jeffrey Leonard, *Natural Resources in Central America* (Washington, D.C.: International Institute of Environment and Development, 1987).

34. Latin American and Caribbean Commission on Development and Environment, *Our Own Agenda* (Washington, D.C.: Inter-American Development Bank and United Nations Development Programme, 1992), 19.

35. Lori Ann Thrupp, "Entrapment and Escape from Fruitless Insecticide Use," *International Journal of Environmental Studies*, 1990, vol. 36:173–189; Lori Ann Thrupp, "Long-term Losses from Accumulation of Pesticide Residues," *Geoforum*, 1991, vol. 22, no. 1:1–15.

36. Jorge Torres, "Agricultural Modernization and Resource Deterioration in Latin America," draft paper, Interamerican Institute for Cooperation on Agriculture, San José, Costa Rica, 1994, p. 7.

See also Douglas Murray and Polly Hoppin, "Recurring Contradictions in Agrarian Development: Pesticide Problems in the Caribbean Basin Nontraditional Agriculture," *World Development*, 1992, vol. 20, no. 4; Bradford Barham, M. Clark, E. Katz, and R. Schurman, "Nontraditional Agricultural Exports in Latin America," *Latin American Research Review*, 1992, vol. 11, no. 26.

37. Bradford Barham, M. Clark, E. Katz, and R. Schurman, "Nontraditional Agricultural Exports in Latin America," *Latin American Research Review*, 1992, vol. 11, no. 26.

38. Jorge Torres, "Agricultural Modernization and Resource Deterioration in Latin America," draft paper, Interamerican Institute for Cooperation on Agriculture, San José, Costa Rica, 1994, p. 26.

39. Panfilo Tabora, "Central America and South America's Pacific Rim Countries: Experience with Export Diversification," in Shawki Barghouti, L. Garbus, and D. Umali, eds., *Trends in Agricultural Diversification*, World Bank Technical Paper number 180 (Washington, D.C.: World Bank, 1992), 95.

40. Panfilo Tabora, "Central America and South America's Pacific Rim Countries: Experience with Export Diversification," in Shawki Barghouti, L. Garbus, and D. Umali, eds., *Trends in Agricultural Diversification*, World Bank Technical Paper number 180 (Washington, D.C.: World Bank, 1992), 95.

41. Panfilo Tabora, "Central America and South America's Pacific Rim Countries: Experience with Export Diversification," in Shawki Barghouti, L. Garbus, and D. Umali, eds., *Trends in Agricultural Diversification*, World Bank Technical Paper number 180 (Washington, D.C.: World Bank, 1992), 95.

42. Jorge Torres, "Agricultural Modernization and Resource Deterioration in Latin America," draft paper, Interamerican Institute for Cooperation on Agriculture, San José, Costa Rica, 1994, p. 55.

43. José Mendez, *The Development of The Colombian Cut Flower Industry*, World Bank Working Paper WPS 660 (Washington, D.C.: World Bank, 1991), 14.

44. José Mendez, *The Development of The Colombian Cut Flower Industry*, World Bank Working Paper Series 660 (Washington, D.C.: World Bank, 1991), 14.

45. Sarah Stewart. "Colombian Flowers: The Gift of Love and Poison." News Release. (London: Christian Aid, 1994.)

46. Jorge Torres, "Agricultural Modernization and Resource Deterioration in Latin America," draft paper, Interamerican Institute for Cooperation on Agriculture, San José, Costa Rica, 1994, p. 27–96.

47. Luis Llambi, "Comparative Advantages and Disadvantages in Latin American Nontraditional Fruit and Vegetable Exports," in Philip McMichael, ed., *The Global Restructuring of Agro-food Systems* (Ithaca, N.Y.: Cornell University, 1994), 203.

48. Eva Paus, "Economic Development in Central America and the Caribbean," in Eva Paus, ed., *Struggle Against Dependence: Nontraditional Export Growth in Central American and the Caribbean* (Boulder, Colo.: Westview Press, 1988); Asociación para el Avance de las Ciencias Sociales and Policy Alternatives for the Caribbean and Central America, *Growing Dilemmas: Guatemala, the Environment, and the Global Economy* (Austin, Tex.: Documentation Exchange, 1992); Laura Reynolds, "Restructuring of Third World AgroExports," in Philip McMichael, ed., *The Global Restructuring of Agro-food Systems* (Ithaca, N.Y.: Cornell University Press, 1994), 223.

49. Proyecto para Exportación Agrícola No-Tradicional (PROEX-ANT), *Reporte Anual, Enero-Diciembre 1991* (Quito, Ecuador: PROEXANT, 1992); U.S. Agency for International Development/Asociación Nacional para Desarrollo de Empresarios/ Federación de Esportadoras de Ecuador and Stanford Research Institute (SRI) International, *Nontraditional Export Expansion in the Central American Region* (Arlington, Va.: SRI International, 1987); Stephen Lack, "Agricultural Crop Diversification and Export Promotion—Final Evaluation," unpublished paper, U.S. Agency for International Development, Latin America and Caribbean Bureau, Center for Development Information and Evaluation, Trade and Investment Workshop, Washington, D.C., 1989. Also, *see* Jorge Torres, "Agricultural Modernization and Resource Deterioration in Latin America," draft paper, Interamerican Institute for Cooperation on Agriculture, San José, Costa Rica, 1994.

50. James Fox, Kenneth Swanberg, and Thomas Mehen, "Agribusiness Assessment: Guatemala Case Study," draft paper, U.S. Agency for International Development, Washington, D.C., 1994.

51. Cited in Margaret Lycette, "Women, Poverty and the Role of USAID," in *Poverty Focus*, Bulletin, no. 2 (Washington, D.C.: Overseas Development Council, 1994), 5.

52. U.S. Agency for International Development, unpublished data, 1993.

53. Proyecto para Exportación Agrícola No-Tradicional (PROEX-ANT), *Reporte Anual, Enero-Diciembre 1991* (Quito, Ecuador: PROEXANT, 1992).

54. U.S. Agency for International Development, data from Environmental and Natural Resources Information Center and Latin America and Caribbean/Rural Development offices, 1993.

55. Lijia Tamaya, Ministerio de Comercio, personal communication, 1992; Cintia Guimaraes, Inter-American Development Bank, personal communication, December 3, 1993; Suraijit Goswami, World Bank, personal communication, June 25, 1993.

56. Pablo de la Torre, personal communication, 1992.

57. Steven Jaffee, *Exporting High-Value Food Commodities: Success Stories from Developing Countries*, World Bank Discussion Papers number 198 (Washington, D.C.: World Bank, 1993), 38; William Friedland, "Global Fresh Fruit and Vegetable System: An Industrial Organization Analysis," in Philip McMichael, ed., *The Global Restructuring of Agro-food Systems* (Ithaca, N.Y.: Cornell University Press, 1994), 175.

58. William Friedland, "The Transnationalization of Agricultural Production: Palimpsest of the Transnational State," *International Journal of Sociology of Agriculture and Food*, 1991, vol. I:48; Luis Llambi, "Latin American Nontraditional Exports," in Philip McMichael, ed., *The Global Restructuring of Agro-food Systems* (Ithaca, N.Y.: Cornell University Press, 1994), 195.

59. U.S. Department of Agriculture; Economic Research Service; cited in Rigoberto Lopez and Leo Polopolus, *Vegetable Markets in the Western Hemisphere* (Ames, Iowa: Iowa State University Press, 1992), 26.

60. Roberta Cook, "Demand Trends in the U.S. Fresh Produce Industry," conference paper, Monterey Bay Economic Outlook Conference, Monterey, Calif., January 23, 1989; cited in Nola Regina Bonis, "NTAEs in Central America: An Analysis of

Costs and Benefits as they Apply to Guatemala", thesis, University of Texas, Austin, Tex., 1990, p. 48.

61. Roberta Cook, "Demand Trends in the U.S. Fresh Produce Industry," conference paper, Monterey Bay Economic Outlook Conference, Monterey, Calif., January 23, 1989; cited in Nola Regina Bonis, "NTAEs in Central America: An Analysis of Costs and Benefits as they Apply to Guatemala", thesis, University of Texas, Austin, Tex., 1990, p. 48.

62. Francisco Stargardter, "The European Market for Central American Produce," conference paper, Second Annual Regional Conference, U.S. Agency for International Development, Regional Office for Central America and Panama, Nontraditional Agricultural Export Support Project, Proyecto para la Exportación Agrícola, Guatemala City, Guatemala, 1989.

63. Polly Hoppin et al., *Pesticide Use in Four Non-traditional Crops in Guatemala: Implications for Residues* (Guatemala City, Guatemala: U.S. Agency for International Development, Regional Office for Central America and Panama), 44.

64. Michael Conroy, "Problemas y alternativas económicas a las EANT," in Institute de Nutrición de Centroamérica y Panamá (INCAP) and World Resources Institute (WRI), *Sostenibilidad de la Producción Agrícola No-Tradicional de Exportación por Pequeños Productores en Guatemala* (Guatemala City, Guatemala: INCAP and WRI, April 1994).

65. Nola Regina Bonis, "NTAEs in Central America: An Analysis of Costs and Benefits as they Apply to Guatemala", thesis, University of Texas, Austin, Tex., 1990, p. 50.

66. Steven Jaffee, *Exporting High-Value Food Commodities: Success Stories from Developing Countries*, World Bank Discussion Papers number 198 (Washington, D.C.: World Bank, 1993), 1.

67. Steven Jaffee, *Exporting High-Value Food Commodities: Success Stories from Developing Countries*, World Bank Discussion Papers number 198 (Washington, D.C.: World Bank, 1993), 1.

68. Martin Raine, "Strategy for the Promotion of Nontraditional Agricultural Exports," internal discussion paper, Latin America and Caribbean Region, World Bank, Washington, D.C.,1989, p. 3.

69. Steven Jaffee, *Exporting High-Value Food Commodities: Success Stories from Developing Countries*, World Bank Discussion Pa-

pers number 198 (Washington, D.C.: World Bank, 1993), 38; William Friedland, "The Global Fresh Fruit and Vegetable System: An Industrial Organization Analysis," in Philip McMichael, ed., *The Global Restructuring of Agro-food Systems* (Ithaca, N.Y.: Cornell University Press, 1994).

70. William Friedland, "The Global Fresh Fruit and Vegetable System: An Industrial Organization Analysis," in Philip McMichael, ed., *The Global Restructuring of Agro-food Systems* (Ithaca, N.Y.: Cornell University Press, 1994), 176.

71. Luis Llambi, "Latin American Nontraditional Exports," in Philip McMichael, ed., *The Global Restructuring of Agro-food Systems* (Ithaca, N.Y.: Cornell University Press, 1994), 195.

72. Steven Jaffee, *Exporting High-Value Food Commodities: Success Stories from Developing Countries*, World Bank Discussion Papers number 198 (Washington, D.C.: World Bank, 1993), 38.

73. U.S. International Trade Commission (USITC), *Report on the Impact of the Caribbean Economic Recovery Act on U.S. Industry Consumers*, Seventh Report of 1991, publication 2553 (Washington, D.C.: USITC, September 1992); U.S. Department of Commerce, *Guidebook to the Andean Trade Preference Act (APTA)* (Washington, D.C.: U.S. Department of Commerce, July 1992).

74. U.S. International Trade Commission (USITC), *Report on the Impact of the Caribbean Economic Recovery Act on U.S. Industry Consumers*, Seventh Report of 1991, publication 2553 (Washington, D.C.: USITC, September 1992); U.S. Department of Commerce, *Guidebook to the Andean Trade Preference Act (APTA)* (Washington, D.C.: U.S. Department of Commerce, July 1992).

75. U.S. International Trade Commission (USITC), *Report on the Impact of the Caribbean Economic Recovery Act on U.S. Industry Consumers*, Seventh Report of 1991, publication 2553 (Washington, D.C.: USITC, September 1992).

76. U.S. International Trade Commission (USITC), *Report on the Impact of the Caribbean Economic Recovery Act on U.S. Industry Consumers*, Seventh Report of 1991, publication 2553 (Washington, D.C.: USITC, September 1992).

77. Anne Krueger, *Economic Policies at Cross Purposes: The United States and Developing Countries* (Washington, D.C.: The Brookings Institution, 1993).

78. U.S. Department of Commerce, *Guidebook to the Andean Trade Preference Act (ATPA)* (Washington, D.C.: U.S. Department of Commerce, July 1992).

79. Luis Llambi, "Latin American Nontraditional Exports," in Philip McMichael, ed., *The Global Restructuring of Agro-food Systems* (Ithaca, N.Y.: Cornell University Press, 1994), 196.

80. James Vertrees and Leo Mayer, "The Uruguay Round of Trade Negotiations: Implications for Trade in Horticultural Products," in Rigoberto Lopez and Leo Polopolus, eds., *Vegetable Markets in the Western Hemisphere* (Ames, Iowa: Iowa State University Press, 1992), 193–200.

81. In Guatemala, for example, the National Plan for NTAE Promotion of 1985–89 is part of the government's broad "Short-term Economic and Social Reorganization Program" (PRES), passed in 1986. [Maarten Immink, E. Kennedy, H. Hahn, E. Payongayong, *Nontraditional Export Crops Among Smallholder Farmers and Production, Income, Nutrition, and Quality of Life Effects: A Comparative Analysis 1985–1991* (Washington, D.C.: International Food Policy Research Institute, 1993)].

82. Proyecto para Exportación Agrícola No-Tradicional (PROEXANT), "Procesos para Exportación de Productos Notradicionales" (video) (Quito, Ecuador: PROEXANT, 1991).

83. Martin Raine, "Strategy for the Promotion of Nontraditional Agricultural Exports," internal discussion paper, Latin America and Caribbean Region, World Bank, Washington, D.C., 1989.

84. For example, in Ecuador, before 1992, in order to export any product, exporters were required to follow numerous bureaucratic procedures, including filling out multiple forms, obtaining hundreds of signatures, and acquiring permits from several agencies—all of which took on average 138 hours per shipment to complete (Proyecto para Exportación Agrícola No-Tradicional, unpublished data, video tape).

85. Steven Jaffee, *Exporting High-Value Food Commodities: Success Stories from Developing Countries*, World Bank Discussion Papers number 198 (Washington, D.C.: World Bank, 1993), 43; G.S. Scobie, *The Impact of Macro-Structural Adjustments on the Poor: Towards a Research Strategy* (Ithaca, N.Y.: Cornell Nutrition and Food Policy Program, 1989).

86. Martin Raine, "Strategy for the Promotion of Nontraditional Agricultural Exports," internal discussion paper, Latin America and Caribbean Region, World Bank, Washington, D.C., 1989; Steven Jaffee, *Exporting High-Value Food Commodities: Success Stories from Developing Countries* (Washington, D.C.: World Bank, 1993. Also, Mauricio Davalos, personal communication, Quito, Ecuador, 1993.

87. Steven Jaffee, *Exporting High-Value Food Commodities: Success Stories from Developing Countries,* World Bank Discussion Papers number 198 (Washington, D.C.: World Bank, 1993), 43; Jorge Torres, "Agricultural Modernization and Resource Deterioration in Latin America," draft paper, Interamerican Institute for Cooperation on Agriculture, San José, Costa Rica, 1994.

88. Maarten Immink et al., *Nontraditional Export Crops Among Smallholder Farmers and Production, Incomes, Nutrition, and Quality of Life Effects: A Comparative Analysis 1985–1991* (Washington, D.C.: International Food Policy Research Institute, 1993).

89. Maarten Immink et al., *Nontraditional Export Crops Among Smallholder Farmers and Production, Income, Nutrition, and Quality of Life Effects: A Comparative Analysis 1985–1991* (Washington, D.C.: International Food Policy Research Institute, 1993).

90. Maarten Immink et al., *Nontraditional Export Crops Among Smallholder Farmers and Production, Income, Nutrition, and Quality of Life Effects: A Comparative Analysis 1985–1991* (Washington, D.C.: International Food Policy Research Institute, 1993).

91. José Mendez, *The Development of the Colombian Cut Flower Industry,* World Bank Working Papers Series 660 (Washington, D.C.: World Bank, 1991); Jorge Torres, "Agricultural Modernization and Resource Deterioration," draft paper, Interamerican Institute for Cooperation on Agriculture, San José, Costa Rica, 1994.

92. Jorge Torres, "Agricultural Modernization and Resource Deterioration," draft paper, Interamerican Institute for Cooperation on Agriculture, San José, Costa Rica, 1994; Steven Jaffee, *Exporting High-Value Food Commodities: Success Stories from Developing Countries,* World Bank Discussion Paper number 198 (Washington, D.C.: World Bank, 1993); interviews with many decision-makers in non-traditional agroexport promotion programs.

93. Jorge Torres, "Agricultural Modernization and Resource Deterioration in Latin America," draft paper, Interamerican Institute for Cooperation on Agriculture, San José, Costa Rica, 1994. An exception was in Guatemala, where the government established a tax policy for both traditional and non-traditional exports, but this tax was not implemented effectively in practice. [Maarten Immink et al., *Nontraditional Export Crops Among Smallholder Farmers and Production, Income, Nutrition, and Quality of Life Effects: A Comparative Analysis 1985–1991* (Washington, D.C.: International Food Policy Research Institute, 1993), 40.]

94. Martin Raine, "Strategy for The Promotion of NonTraditional Agricultural Exports," internal discussion paper, Latin America and Caribbean Region, World Bank, Washington, D.C.: World Bank, 1989, p. 15.

95. Maarten Immink et al., *Nontraditional Export Crops Among Smallholder Farmers and Production, Income, Nutrition, and Quality of Life Effects: A Comparative Analysis 1985–1991* (Washington, D.C.: International Food Policy Research Institute, 1993), 40.

96. Martin Raine, "Strategy for The Promotion of NonTraditional Agricultural Exports," internal discussion paper, Latin America and Caribbean Region, World Bank, Washington, D.C., 1989, p. 15.

97. Maarten Immink et al., *Nontraditional Export Crops Among Smallholder Farmers and Production, Incomes, Nutrition, and Quality of Life Effects: A Comparative Analysis 1985–1991* (Washington, D.C.: International Food Policy Research Institute, 1993), 39.

98. Pablo de la Torre, personal communication, 1993; Cintia Guimares, Inter-American Development Bank, personal communication, 1993.

99. Ecuadorian bank officials, personal communications, 1993.

100. Latin American and Caribbean Comission on Development and Environment, *Our Own Agenda* (Washington, D.C.: Inter-American Development Bank and United Nations Development Programme, 1991); World Resources Institute (WRI) and U.S. Agency for International Development (USAID), *Green*

Guidance for Latin America and the Caribbean: Integrating Environmental Concerns in USAID Programming (Washington, D.C.: WRI and USAID, 1993).

101. Sources of information include Douglas Murray, *Cultivating Crisis: The Human Costs of Pesticides in Central America* (Austin, Tex.: University of Texas Press, 1994); David Bull, *A Growing Problem: Pesticides and the Third World Poor* (Oxford: Oxfam, 1982); Lori Ann Thrupp, "Pesticides and Policies: Approaches to Pest Control Dilemmas in Nicaragua and Costa Rica," *Latin American Perspectives*, Fall 1988, issue 59, vol. 15, no. 4; Robert Boardman, *Pesticides in World Agriculture: The Politics of International Regulation* (London, England: MacMillan, 1986).

102. Robert Repetto, *Paying the Price: Pesticide Subsidies in Developing Countries*, Research Report #2 (Washington, D.C.: World Resources Institute, 1985); Lori Ann Thrupp, "Inappropriate Incentives for Pesticide Use: Agricultural Credit Requirements in Developing Countries," *Agriculture and Human Values*, Summer-Fall 1990:62–69.

103. U.S. Agency for International Development, Latin America and Caribbean Bureau, Environment Office, "Environmental Impact Evaluations for Non-traditional Export Promotion Programs," for Central America, Ecuador, and Caribbean countries, unpublished.

104. Interviews with Proyecto para la Exportación Agrícola officers and a U.S. Agency for International Development officer, 1993/94.

105. U.S. Food and Drug Administration (USFDA), *Requirements of Laws and Regulations Enforced by the U.S. Food and Drug Administration* (Rockville, Md.: U.S. Department of Health and Human Services, Food and Drug Administration, 1984), 9–39; Nicholas Powers and Richard Heifner, *Federal Grade Standards for Fresh Produce: Linkages to Pesticide Use*, Economic Research Service bulletin number 675 (Washington, D.C.: U.S. Department of Agriculture, 1993).

106. National Research Council, *Alternative Agriculture* (Washington, D.C.: National Academy Press, 1989), 126.

107. Kenneth Swanberg, "Evaluation Highlight: Agribusiness Assessment, Nontraditional Agricultural Export in Ecuador,"

unpublished report, U.S. Agency for International Development, Center for Development Information and Evaluation, Washington, D.C., 1994, p. 1.

108. Interviews with non-traditional agroexport program officers in Ecuador, Guatemala, and Costa Rica, 1993.

109. Steven Jaffee, *Exporting High-Value Food Commodities: Success Stories from Developing Countries*, World Bank Discussion Papers number 198 (Washington, D.C.: World Bank, 1993), 38; William Friedland, "Global Fresh Fruit and Vegetable System: An Industrial Organization Analysis," in Philip McMichael, ed., *The Global Restructuring of Agro-food Systems* (Ithaca, N.Y.: Cornell University Press, 1994), 175. Also based on field interviews, 1993.

110. Steven Jaffee, *Exporting High-Value Food Commodities: Success Stories from Developing Countries*, World Bank Discussion Paper number 198 (Washington, D.C.: World Bank, 1993), 1.

111. Steven Jaffee, *Exporting High-Value Food Commodities: Success Stories from Developing Countries* (Washington, D.C.: World Bank, 1993), vii and 6; Luis Llambi, "Latin American Nontraditional Exports," in Philip McMichael, ed., *The Global Restructuring of Agro-food Systems* (Ithaca, N.Y.: Cornell University Press, 1994); field interviews in Ecuador and Guatemala.

112. In the United States, 14 federal and 29 state marketing orders regulated fresh produce in 1987. David Mares, *Penetrating the International Market: Theoretical Considerations and a Mexican Case Study* (New York, N.Y.: Colombia University Press, 1987), 205; cited in Luis Llambi, "Latin American Nontraditional Exports," in Philip McMichael, ed., *The Global Restructuring of Agro-food Systems* (Ithaca, N.Y.: Cornell University Press, 1994), 197.

113. Odin Knudsen and John Nash, *Redefining the Government's Role in Agriculture in the Nineties* (Washington, D.C.: World Bank, 1990); cited in Luis Llambi, "Latin American Nontraditional Exports," in Philip McMichael, ed., *The Global Restructuring of Agro-food Systems* (Ithaca, N.Y.: Cornell University Press, 1994), 196; and meeting with melon producers in Guayaquil, 1993.

114. Information from U.S. Department of Agriculture, *Chemonics Guide to Regulations*, and Robert Bailey, personal communica-

tion, 1993. Also *see* Nola Regina Bonis, "The Nontraditional Agricultural Production Strategy in Central America," thesis, University of Texas, Austin, Tex., 1990.

115. For non-traditional agroexports to Europe, three basic documents are usually required upon entry: 1) phytosanitary certificate; 2) commercial invoice that indicates details of the shipment; and 3) certificate of origin. (U.S. Department of Agriculture data cited in Agricultural and Rural Development Technical Services Project/U.S. Agency for International Development guide to regulations). Robert Bailey, "Requisitos Sobre Residuos y Calidad," in *Désafios en la Agroexportación Notradicional: Impactos Ambientales y Sociales* (Quito, Ecuador: Universidad San Francisco de Quito and World Resources Institute, 1993).

116. U.S. Department of Agriculture marketing regulations; Fredda Valenti, personal communication, April 1994.

117. Based on interviews with decision-makers in Ecuador, Guatemala, and Costa Rica, and corroborated in Shawki Barghouti et al., *Trends in Agricultural Diversification: Regional Perspectives*, World Bank Technical Paper number 180 (Washington, D.C.: World Bank, 1993).

118. Panfilo Tabora, "Central America and South America's Pacific Rim Countries: Experience with Export Diversification," in Shawki Barghouti, L. Garbus, and D. Umali, eds., *Trends in Agricultural Diversification: Regional Perspectives*, World Bank Technical Paper number 180 (Washington, D.C.: World Bank, 1992), 99.

119. Andrés Achong, "Alcances y limitaciones de las exportaciones agrícolas no tradicionales," in Ana Beatriz Mendizábal P. and Jürgen Weller, eds., *Promesa o Espejismo?* (Panama City, Panama: Programa Regional del Empleo para América Latina y el Caribe, 1992), 397; Proyecto para Exportación Agrícola No-Tradicional, unpublished data, Quito, Ecuador.

120. Michael Carter, Bradford Barham, Dina Mesbah, and Denise Stanley, "Agroexports and the Rural Resource Poor in Latin America: Policy Options for Achieving Broadly-Based Growth," draft paper, University of Wisconsin, Land Tenure Center, Madison, Wis., 1993.

121. Joachim von Braun, David Hotchkiss, and Maarten Immink, *Nontraditional Export Crops in Guatemala: Effects on Production, Income and Nutrition* (Washington, D.C.: International Food Policy Research Institute, 1989); Instituto de Nutrición de Centro América y Panamá.

122. Michael Carter, Bradford Barham, Dina Mesbah, and Denise Stanley, "Agroexports and the Rural Resource Poor in Latin America: Policy Options for Achieving Broadly-Based Growth," draft paper, University of Wisconsin, Land Tenure Center, Madison, Wis., 1993.

123. Steven Jaffee, *Exporting High-Value Food Commodities: Success Stories from Developing Countries*, World Bank Discussion Papers number 198 (Washington, D.C.: World Bank, 1993), 7.

124. Steven Jaffee, *Exporting High-Value Food Commodities: Success Stories from Developing Countries*, World Bank Discussion Papers number 198 (Washington, D.C.: World Bank, 1993), 7.

125. Michael Carter, Bradford Barham, Dina Mesbah, and Denise Stanley, "Agroexports and the Rural Resource Poor in Latin America: Policy Options for Achieving Broadly-Based Growth," draft paper, University of Wisconsin, Land Tenure Center, Madison, Wis., 1993.

126. Michael Carter, Bradford Barham, Dina Mesbah, and Denise Stanley, "Agroexports and the Rural Resource Poor in Latin America: Policy Options for Achieving Broadly-Based Growth," draft paper, University of Wisconsin, Land Tenure Center, Madison, Wis., 1993, p. 13. Also, for details on this point, *see* David Glover and Ken Kusterer, *Small Farmers, Big Business: Contract Farming and Rural Development* (New York, N.Y.: St. Martin's Press, 1990).

127. These features have been described for traditional agroexport systems as well. *See*, e.g., David Goodman and Michael Redclift, "The Machinery of Hunger: the Crisis of Latin American Food Systems," *Environment and Development in Latin America: the Politics of Sustainability* (Manchester: Manchester University Press, 1991).

128. Ian Merwin and Marvin Pritts, "Are Modern Fruit Production Systems Sustainable?," *HortTechnology*, April-June 1993, vol. 3, no. 2:130.

129. *See, e.g.,* Richard W. Fisher, Roberto Cáceres, Edgardo Cáceres, and Danilo Ardón, "Informe Final: Evaluación del Manejo de Plagas y Plaguicidas en Arveja China del Altiplano de Guatemala," unpublished final report on study by Centro Mesoamericano de Tecnología Apropiada, El Instituto de Ciencia y Tecnología Agrícola, and World Resources Institute, Guatemala City, Guatemala, April 1994; Proyecto para Exportación Agrícola No-Tradicional and Universidad San Francisco de Quito, unpublished survey of pesticide use, Quito, Ecuador; Douglas Murray, *Cultivating Crisis: The Human Cost of Pesticides in Central America* (Austin, Tex.: University of Texas Press, 1994).

130. Douglas Murray and Polly Hoppin, "Recurring Contradictions in Agrarian Development: Pesticide Problems in the Caribbean Basin Nontraditional Agriculture," *World Development,* 1992, vol. 20, no. 4:603; Ian Merwin and Marvin Pritts, "Are Modern Fruit Production Systems Sustainable?," *HortTechnology,* April-June 1993, vol. 3, no. 2:131. Also AGROSTAT data from the Food and Agriculture Organization, Rome, Italy.

131. The factors identified here have been verified through field interviews and analysis of farmer decision-making.

132. Adapted from Ian Merwin and Marvin Pritts, "Are Modern Fruit Production Systems Sustainable?," *HortTechnology,* April-June 1993, vol. 3, no. 2:129; T.E. Crews, C.L. Mohler, and A.G. Power, "Energetics and Ecosystem Integrity: The Defining Principles of Sustainable Agriculture," *American Journal of Alternative Agriculture,* 1992, vol. 6:146–149; and Gordon Conway, "Agroecosystem Analysis," *Agricultural Administration,* 1985, vol. 20:31–55.

133. Roberta Von Haeften et al., "LAC Developmental Trends; Background for New Strategy," unpublished data tables for Officers' Workshop, U.S. Agency for International Development, Latin America and Caribbean Bureau, Washington, D.C., 1993. This figure is based on a broad definition of nontraditional agroexports, which includes nuts, pulses, and oils, as well as the fruits, vegetables, and flowers that are the focus of this study.

134. U.S. Agency for International Development statistics cited in Douglas Murray, *Cultivating Crisis: The Human Cost of Pesticides* (Austin, Tex.: University of Texas Press, 1994), 60.
135. Michael Carter, Bradford Barham, Dina Mesbah, and Denise Stanley, "Agroexports and the Rural Resource Poor in Latin America: Policy Options for Achieving Broadly-Based Growth," draft paper, University of Wisconsin, Land Tenure Center, Madison, Wis., 1993, p. 5.
136. Kenneth Swanberg, "Agribusiness Assessment: NTAEs in Ecuador," draft paper, U.S. Agency for International Development, Center for Development Information and Evaluation, Washington, D.C., 1994 (based on data from Proyecto para Exportación Agrícola No-Tradicional, Quito, Ecuador).
137. World Resources Institute analysis, based on U.S. Department of Agriculture, Economic Marketing Service, unpublished data, 1994.
138. Proyecto para Exportación Agrícola No-Tradicional (PROEX-ANT), *Reporte Anual, Enero-Deciembre 1991* (Quito, Ecuador: PROEXANT, 1992); and Banco Central, unpublished data, 1992.
139. Proyecto para la Exportación Agrícola, 1993; unpublished data cited in Richard Fisher, Roberto Cáceres, Edgardo Cáceras, and Danilo Ardon, "Evaluación del Manejo de Plagas y Plaguicidas en Arveja China del Altiplano de Guatemala," unpublished final report, Centro Mesoamericano de Technolgía Apropriada, Instituto de Ciencia y Tecnología Agrícola, and World Resources Institute, Guatemala City, Guatemala, 1994.
140. Proyecto para la Exportación Agrícola, 1993; unpublished data cited in Richard Fisher, Roberto Cáceres, Edgardo Cáceras, and Danilo Ardon, "Evaluación del Manejo de Plagas y Plaguicidas en Arveja China del Altiplano de Guatemala," unpublished final report, Centro Mesoamericano de Tecnología Apropriada, Instituto de Ciencia y Tecnología Agrícola, and World Resources Institute, Guatemala City, Guatemala, 1994.
141. U.S. Department of Agriculture (USDA), *Foreign Agricultural Trade of the United States (FATUS)* (Washington, D.C.: USDA, Economic Research Service, 1993).

142. Proyecto para Exportación Agrícola No-Tradicional (PROEX-ANT), *Reporte Anual, Enero-Deciembre 1991* (Quito, Ecuador: PROEXANT, 1992); Banco Central, unpublished data, 1992.

143. Michael Carter, Bradford Barham, Dina Mesbah, and Denise Stanley, "Agroexports and the Rural Resource Poor in Latin America: Policy Options for Achieving Broadly-Based Growth," draft paper, University of Wisconsin, Land Tenure Center, Madison, Wis., 1993, p. 5.

144. James Fox, K. Swanberg, and T. Mehen, "Agribusiness Assessment: The Case of Guatemala," draft paper, U.S. Agency for International Development, Washington, D.C., 1994, p. 12.

145. Andrés Achong, "Alcances y limitaciones de las exporta-ciones agrícolas no tradicionales," in Ana Beatriz Mendizábal P. and Jürgen Weller, eds., *Promesa o Espejismo?* (Panama City, Panama: Programa Regional del Empleo para América Latina y el Caribe, 1992), 398.

146. Andrés Achong, "Alcances y limitaciones de las exporta-ciones agrícolas no tradicionales," in Ana Beatriz Mendizábal P. and Jürgen Weller, eds., *Promesa o Espejismo?* (Panama City, Panama: Programa Regional del Empleo para América Latina y el Caribe, 1992), 398.

147. Andrés Achong, "Alcances y limitaciones de las exporta-ciones agrícolas no tradicionales," in Ana Beatriz Mendizábal P. and Jürgen Weller, eds., *Promesa o Espejismo?* (Panama City, Panama: Programa Regional del Empleo para América Latina y el Caribe, 1992), 398.

148. Luis Gomez Osorio, Walter Chamochumbi, and Kees Van De Burg, *Las Flores: Un Callejón Sin Salida?* (Lima, Perú: JLP Impresores and Red de Acción en Alternativas al Uso de Agroquímicos, 1992), 44.

149. Joaquim Von Braun, D. Hotchkiss, and M. Immink, *Nontraditional Export Crops in Guatemala: Effects on Production, Income and Nutrition* (Washington, D.C.: International Food Policy Research Institute, 1989).

150. James Fox, K. Swanberg, and T. Mehen, "Agribusiness Assessment: The Case of Guatemala," draft paper, U.S. Agency for International Development, Washington, D.C., 1994, p. 12.

151. James Fox, K. Swanberg, and T. Mehen, "Agribusiness As-

sessment: The Case of Guatemala," draft paper, U.S. Agency for International Development, Washington, D.C., 1994, p. 35.

152. José Mendez, *The Development of the Colombian Cut Flower Industry*, World Bank Working Paper Series 660 (Washington, D.C.: World Bank, Country Economics Department, 1991), 12.

153. Proyecto para Exportación Agrícola No-Tradicional, unpublished information; Jorge Rodriguez, personal communication, 1993.

154. William F. Waters, "Las agroexportaciones como respuesta a las transformaciones fordistas mundiales," in A. Mauro, ed., *Latino America Agraria Hacia el Siglo XXI* (Quito: Centro de Planificación y Estudios Sociales). 161–181.

155. Panfilo Tabora, "Central America and South America's Pacific Rim Countries: Experience with Export Diversification," in Shawki Barghouti, L. Garbus, and D. Umali, eds., *Trends in Agricultural Diversification*, World Bank Technical Paper number 180 (Washington, D.C.: World Bank, 1994), 95; Steven Jaffee, *Exporting High Value Food Commodities: Success Stories from Developing Countries*, World Bank Discussion Paper number 198 (Washington, D.C.: World Bank, 1993); field data.

156. Shawki Barghouti, L. Garbus, and D. Umali, eds., *Trends in Agricultural Diversification*, World Bank Technical Paper number 180 (Washington, D.C.: World Bank, 1994), 94.

157. Panfilo Tabora, "Central America and South America's Pacific Rim Countries: Experience with Export Diversification," in Shawki Barghouti, L. Garbus, and D. Umali, eds., *Trends in Agricultural Diversification*, World Bank Technical Paper number 180 (Washington, D.C.: World Bank, 1992), 94.

158. Shawki Barghouti, L. Garbus, and D. Umali, eds., *Trends in Agricultural Diversification*, World Bank Technical Paper number 180 (Washington, D.C.: World Bank, 1994), 101.

159. Simon Maxwell and Adrian Fernando. "Cash Crops in Developing Countries: The Issues, the Facts, the Policies," *World Development*, 1989. vol. 17 no. 11: 1679. Bradford Barham, M. Clark, E. Katz, and R. Schurman. "Nontraditional Agricultural Exports in Latin America," *Latin America Research Review*, 1992, vol. 11 no. 26: 51–53

160. For examples, see Rati Ram, "Exports and Economic Growth in Developing Countries: Evidence from Time-Series and Cross-Section Cata." *Economic Development and Cultural Change*, 1987, vol. 36, no. 1: 51–72. Bela Balassa, "Export Incentives and Export Performance in Developing Economies," *Weltwirtschaftlichers Archiv*, 1978. no. 114: 24–61. cited in Bradford Barham, M. Clark, E. Katz, and R. Schurman, "Nontraditional Agricultural Exports in Latin America," *Latin America Research Review*, 1992, vol. 11, no. 26.

161. Bradford Barham, M. Clark, E. Katz, and R. Schurman, "Nontraditional Agricultural exports in Latin America," *Latin America Research Review*, 1992. vol 11., no. 26: 51–52. Krishna Kumar, personal communication, December 1994. Michael Carter, personal communication, December 1994.

162. Davalos Mauricio, Marco Penaherrera, and Pablo de la Torre, personal communications, 1993. See also Ana Beatriz Mendizábal P. and Jürgen Weller, eds., *Promesa o Espejismo?* (Panama City, Panama: Programa Regional del Empleo para América Latina y el Caribe, 1992); Jorge Torres, "Agricultural Modernization and Resource Deterioration in Latin America," draft paper, Interamerican Institute for Cooperation on Agriculture, San José, Costa Rica, 1994.

163. See, e.g., Bradford Barham, M. Clark, E. Katz, and R. Schurman, "Nontraditional Agricultural Exports in Latin America," *Latin American Research Review*, 1992, vol. 11, no. 26; Nola Regina Bonis, "The Nontraditional Agricultural Production Strategy in Central America," thesis, University of Texas, Austin, Tex., 1990.

164. Bradford Barham, M. Clark, E. Katz, and R. Schurman, "Nontraditional Agricultural Exports in Latin America," *Latin American Research Review*, 1992, vol. 11, no. 26.

165. See e.g., Steven Jaffee, *Exporting High-Value Food Commodities: Success Stories from Developing Countries*, World Bank Discussion Paper number 198 (Washington, D.C.: World Bank, 1992).

166. Amy Sparks and Boris Bravo-Ureta. "Fruit Production in Chile: A Review of Recent Developments." *Journal of International Food and Agribusiness Marketing*. 4(4), 1992: 57.

167. Bradford Barham, M. Clark, E. Katz, and R. Schurman, "Nontraditional Agricultural Exports in Latin America," *Latin American Research Review*, 1992, vol. 11, no. 26.

168. David Kaimowitz, *El Apoyo Necesario para Promover las Exportaciones Agrícolas No Tradicionales en América Central*, documento número 30 (San José, Costa Rica: Interamerican Institute for Cooperation on Agriculture, 1992), 13. Also sec Joseph Collins, "Nontraditional Agroexports, Basic Food Crops, and Small Farmers in Central America," unpublished paper, Inter-American Foundation, Arlington, Va., 1992, p. 7.

169. David Kaimowitz, *El Apoyo Necesario para Promover las Exportaciones Agrícolas No Tradicionales en América Central*, documento número 30 (San José, Costa Rica: Interamerican Institute for Cooperation on Agriculture, 1992), 14.

170. David Kaimowitz, *El Apoyo Necesario para Promover las Exportaciones Agrícolas No Tradicionales en América Central*, documento número 30 (San José, Costa Rica: Interamerican Institute for Cooperation on Agriculture, 1992), 14.

171. Bradford Barham, M. Clark, E. Katz, and R. Schurman, "Nontraditional Agricultural Exports in Latin America," *Latin American Research Review*, 1992, vol. 11, no. 26.

172. Bradford Barham, M. Clark, E. Katz, and R. Schurman, "Nontraditional Agricultural Exports in Latin America," *Latin American Research Review*, 1992, vol. 11, no. 26.

173. Joseph Collins, "Nontraditional Agroexports, Basic Food Crops, and Small Farmers in Central America," unpublished paper, Inter-American Foundation, Arlington, Va., 1992, p. 8; Bradford Barham, M. Clark, E. Katz, and R. Schurman, "Nontraditional Agricultural Exports in Latin America," *Latin American Research Review*, 1992, vol. 11, no. 26.

174. David Kaimowitz, *El Apoyo Necesario para Promover las Exportaciones Agrícolas No Tradicionales en América Central*, documento número 30 (San José, Costa Rica: Interamerican Institute for Cooperation on Agriculture, 1992), 14.

175. David Kaimowitz, *El Apoyo Necesario para Promover las Exportaciones Agrícolas No Tradicionales en América Central*, documento número 30 (San José, Costa Rica: Interamerican Institute for Cooperation on Agriculture, 1992), 15.

176. James Fox, K. Swanberg, and T. Mehen, "Agribusiness Assessment: The Case of Guatemala," draft paper, U.S. Agency
for International Development, Washington, D.C., 1994, p. 12.

177. William F. Waters, "Restructuring of Ecuadorian Agriculture
and the Development of Nontraditional Exports: Evidence
from the Cut Flower Industry," (Quito: Universidad San Francisco de Quito, 1992). (Paper presented at the 55th Meeting of
the Rural Sociological Society, University Park, PA.)

178. David Kaimowitz, *El Apoyo Necesario para Promover las Exportaciones Agrícolas No Tradicionales en América Central*, documento número 30 (San José, Costa Rica: Interamerican Institute for Cooperation on Agriculture, 1992), 15.

179. Michael Carter, B. Barhan, D. Mesbah, and D. Stanley,
"Agroexports and the Rural Resource Poor in Latin America:
Policy Options for Achieving Broadly-Based Economic
Growth," unpublished paper, University of Wisconsin, Land
Tenure Center, Madison, Wis., 1993, pp. 17 and C-1.

180. Michael Carter, B. Barham, D. Mesbah, and D. Stanley,
"Agroexports and the Rural Resource Poor in Latin America:
Policy Options for Achieving Broadly-Based Economic
Growth," unpublished paper, University of Wisconsin, Land
Tenure Center, Madison, Wis., 1993, pp. 20–21 and A-1.

181. *See* e.g., Michael Carter, B. Barham, D. Mesbah, and D. Stanley,
"Agroexports and the Rural Resource Poor in Latin America,"
unpublished paper, University of Wisconsin, Land Tenure Cen-
ter, Madison, Wis., 1993; Instituto de Nutrición de Centro
América y Panamá (INCAP) and World Resources Institute
(WRI), *Sostenabilidad de la Producción Agrícola No-Tradicional de
Exportación por Pequeños Productores en Guatemala* (Guatemala
City, Guatemala: INCAP and WRI, April 1994); Policy Alterna-
tives for the Caribbean and Central America (PACCA) and Aso-
ciación para el Avance de las Ciencias Sociales, *Growing Dilemmas: Guatemala, the Environment, and the Global Economy*
(Washington, D.C.: PACCA, 1992); Michael Conroy, Douglas
Murray and p. Rosset, "Fruits of The Crisis: Gambling on Non-
traditional Agriculture," unpublished book manuscript, 1994;
Douglas Murray, *Cultivating Crisis: The Human Cost of Pesticides
in Central America* (Austin, Tex.: University of Texas Press, 1994).

182. Michael Carter, B. Barham, and D. Mesbah. "Agroexport Booms and the Rural Resource Poor in Chile, Guatemala, and Paraguay." Unpublished paper. (Madison: University of Wisconsin, 1994.) p. 15

183. Michael Carter, B. Barham, and D. Mesbah. "Agroexport Booms and the Rural Resource Poor in Chile, Guatemala, and Paraguay." Unpublished paper. (Madison: University of Wisconsin, 1994.) p. 24

184. *See* e.g., Michael Carter, B. Barham, D. Mesbah, and D. Stanley, "Agroexports and the Rural Resource Poor in Latin America: Policy Options for Achieving Broadly-based Economic Growth," unpublished paper, University of Wisconsin, Land Tenure Center, Madison, Wis., 1993; Instituto de Nutrición de Centro América y Panamá (INCAP) and World Resources Institute (WRI), *Sostenabilidad de la Producción Agrícola No-Tradicional de Exportación por Pequeños Productores en Guatemala* (Guatemala City, Guatemala: INCAP and WRI, 1994); Policy Alternatives for the Caribbean and Central America (PACCA) and Asociación para el Avance de las Ciencias Sociales, *Growing Dilemmas: Guatemala, the Environment, and the Global Economy* (Washington, D.C.: PACCA, 1992); Michael Conway, Doug Murray and P. Rosset, "Fruits of The Crisis," unpublished book manuscript; Douglas Murray, *Cultivating Crisis: The Human Cost of Pesticides in Central America* (Austin, Tex.: University of Texas Press, 1994).

185. Amy Sparks and Bravo-Ureta, "Fruit Production in Chile: A Review of Recent Developments," *Journal of International Food and Agribusiness Marketing*, 1992, vol. 2, no. 4:57.

186. Marco Penaherrera, Proyecto para Exportación Agrícola No-Tradicional, personal communication, 1993.

187. Pablo de la Torre and Lijia Tamaja, bank/credit managers, Proyecto para Exportación Agrícola No-Tradicional, personal communications, Quito, Ecuador, 1993.

188. James Fox, K. Swanberg, and T. Mehan, "Agribusiness Assessment: The Case of Guatemala," draft paper, U.S. Agency for International Development, Washington, D.C., 1994, p. 12.

189. Richard Fisher, Roberto Cáceres, and Danilo Ardon, "Evaluación del Manejo de Plagas y Plaguicidas en Arveja China del

Altiplano de Guatemala," unpublished final report, Centro Mesoamericano de Tecnología Apropriada, Instituto de Ciencia y Tecnología Agrícola, and World Resources Institute, Guatemala City, Guatemala, 1994.

190. James Fox, K. Swanberg, and T. Mehan, "Agribusiness Assessment: The Case of Guatemala," draft paper, U.S. Agency for International Development, Washington, D.C., 1994, p. 30.

191. Proyecto para la Exportación Agrícola, unpublished data, 1993.

192. Maarten Immink et al., *Nontraditional Export Crops Among Smallholder Farmers and Production, Income, Nutrition, and Quality of Life Effects* (Washington, D.C.: International Food Policy Research Institute, 1993), 52.

193. Joaquim Von Braun, D. Hotchkiss, and M. Immink, *Nontraditional Export Crops in Guatemala: Effects on Production, Income and Nutrition* (Washington, D.C.: International Food Policy Research Institute, 1989).

194. Michael Conroy, "Problemas y alternativas económicas a las EANTs," in Instituto de Nutrición de Centroamérica y Panamá (INCAP) and World Resources Institute (WRI), *Sostenabilidad de la Producción Agrícola No-Tradicional de Exportación por Pequeños Productores en Guatemala* (Guatemala City, Guatemala: INCAP and WRI, April 1994). Also, see conclusions from this document (proceedings of workshop).

195. Kevin Healy, personal communication, June 1994.

196. Joaquim Von Braun, D. Hotchkiss, and M. Immink, *Nontraditional Export Crops in Guatemala: Effects on Production, Income and Nutrition* (Washington, D.C.: International Food Policy Research Institute, 1989); P. Rosset, "Sustainability, Economies of Scale, and Social Instability: Achilles Heel of Nontraditional Export Agriculture?", *Agriculture and Human Values*, 1991, vol. 8, no. 3.

197. Michael Conroy, "Problemas y alternativas económicas a las EANTs," in Instituto de Nutrición de Centroamérica y Panamá (INCAP) and World Resources Institute (WRI), *Sostenabilidad de la Producción Agrícola No-Tradicional de Exportación por Pequeños Productores en Guatemala* (Guatemala City, Guatemala: INCAP and WRI, April 1994).

198. Krishna Kumar. *Generating Broad-Based Growth Through Agribusiness Promotion.* USAID Program and Operations Assessment Report No 9. (Washington, D.C.: U.S. Agency for International Development, 1994), p. 33.

199. Mauricio Davalos, personal communication, 1993, and Rafael Arroyo, personal communication, 1993.

200. Michael Carter, B. Barham, and D. Mesbah. "Agroexport Booms and the Rural Resource Poor in Chile, Guatemala, and Paraguay." Unpublished paper. (Madison: University of Wisconsin, 1994.) p. 15

201. Marcelo Mucía, "Sostenabilidad social: la experiencia de los productores de Patzún, Chimaltenango," in Instituto de Nutrición de Centroamérica y Panamá (INCAP) and World Resources Institute (WRI), *Sostenibilidad de la Producción Agrícola No-Tradicional de Exportación por Pequeños Productores en Guatemala* (Guatemala City, Guatemala: INCAP and WRI, April 1994).

202. Data from the National Snow Pea Committee, and DIGESA, Guatemala, via Richard Fisher, personal communication, July 1994; and retail supermarkets in Washington, D.C., 1994.

203. Michael Conroy, "Problemas y alternativas económicas a las EANTs," in Instituto de Nutrición de Centro América y Panamá (INCAP) and World Resources Institute (WRI), *Sostenabilidad de la Producción Agrícola No-Tradicional de Exportación por Pequeños Productores en Guatemala* (Guatemala City, Guatemala: INCAP and WRI, April 1994).

204. Michael Conroy, "Problemas y alternativas económicas a las EANTs," in Instituto de Nutrición de Centro América y Panamá (INCAP) and World Resources Institute (WRI), *Sostenabilidad de la Producción Agrícola No-Tradicional de Exportación por Pequeños Productores en Guatemala* (Guatemala City, Guatemala: INCAP and WRI, April 1994).

205. Michael Conroy, "Problemas y alternativas económicas a las EANTs," in Instituto de Nutrición de Centro América y Panamá (INCAP) and World Resources Institute (WRI), *Sostenabilidad de la Producción Agrícola No-Tradicional de Exportación por Pequeños Productores en Guatemala* (Guatemala City, Guatemala: INCAP and WRI, April 1994).

206. Joaquim von Braun, D. Hotchkiss, and M. Immink, *Nontraditional Export Crops in Guatemala: Effects on Production, Income and Nutrition* (Washington, D.C.: International Food Policy Research Institute, 1989).

207. Elizabeth Katz, "The Impact of Nontraditional Agriculture on Food Expenditures and Consumption in the Guatemalan Central Highlands: An Intra-household Perspective," *Food and Nutrition Bulletin*, December 1993-January 1994, vol. 15, no. 4. Also, see Elizabeth Katz, "Mujeres y trabajo en cultivos no-traditionales," in Instituto de Nutrición de Centro América y Panamá (INCAP) and World Resources Institute (WRI), *Sostenabilidad de la Producción Agrícola No-Traditional de Exportación por Pequeños Productores en Guatemala* (Guatemala City, Guatemala: INCAP and WRI, April 1994).

208. Elizabeth Katz, "Mujeres y trabajo en cultivos no-tradicionales," in Instituto de Nutrición de Centro América y Panamá (INCAP) and World Resources Institute (WRI), *Sostenabilidad de la Producción Agrícola No-Traditional de Exportación por Pequeños Productores en Guatemala* (Guatemala City, Guatemala: INCAP and WRI, April 1994).

209. Elizabeth Katz, "Mujeres y trabajo en cultivos no-tradicionales," in Instituto de Nutrición de Centro América y Panamá and World Resources Institute (WRI), *Sostenabilidad de la Producción Agrícola No-Tradicional de Exportación por Pequeños Productores en Guatemala* (Guatemala City, Guatemala: INCAP and WRI, April 1994).

210. Gilles Bergeron, "Agrarian Structure and the Organization of Peasant Households: A Comparison of Two Guatemalan Ladino Villages," Ph.D. dissertation (Ithaca, N.Y.: Cornell University, 1994).

211. B. Suárez, D. Barkin, B. DeWalt, M. Hernández and R. Rosales. "The nutritional impact of rural modernization: strategies for smallholder survival," *Food and Nutrition Bulletin* 9(3) 1987, 30–35; and B. DeWalt, K. DeWalt, J.C. Escudero, and D. Barkin, "Agrarian reform and small-farmer welfare: evidence from four Mexican communities." *Food and Nutrition Bulletin* 9(3) 1987, 46–52.

212. Results of workshop discussions in Guatemala and Ecuador, and personal communication with producers, 1993.

213. For an overview of literature on this issue, see Simon Maxwell and Adrian Fernando, "Cash Crops in Developing Countries: the Issues, the Facts, the Policies," *World Development*, 1992, vol. 17, no. 11.

214. David Goodman and Michael Redclift, "The Machinery of Hunger in Latin America," in D. Goodman and M. Redclift, *Environment and Development in Latin America* (Manchester: Manchester University Press, 1992); and B. Suárez, D. Barkin, M. Hernández and R. Rosales, "The nutritional impact of rural modernization: strategies for smallholder survival," *Food and Nutrition Bulletin* 9(3) 1987: 30–35. (Also refer to M. Carter et. al in Endnote 228.)

215. See, e.g., B. Barham, M. Clark, E. Katz, and R. Schurman, "Nontraditional Agricultural Exports in Latin America," *Latin American Research Review*, 1992, vol. 11, no. 26; and R.C. Williams, *Export Agriculture and the Crisis in Central America.* (Chapel Hill, N.C.: University of North Carolina Press, 1986.)

216. Michael Carter, Bradford Barham, Dina Mesbah, and Denise Stanley, "Agroexports and the Rural Resource Poor in Latin America: Policy Options for Achieving Broadly-Based Growth," draft paper, University of Wisconsin, Land Tenure Center, Madison, Wisconsin, 1993, p. 5.

217. James Fox, K. Swanberg, and T. Mehan, "Agribusiness Assessment: The Case of Guatemala," draft paper, U.S. Agency for International Development, Washington, D.C., 1994, p. 12.

218. William F. Waters, "Rosas y Claveles: Reestructuraciones en la Producción de Flores," Working Paper No. 5, (Quito: Universidad San Francisco de Quito, 1991; José Mendez, *The Development of the Colombian Cut Flower Industry*, World Bank Working Paper Series 660 (Washington, D.C.: World Bank, Country Economics Department, 1991).

219. Rafael Urriola, "Los Efectos del Crecimiento de la Agroindustria Ecuatoriana y el Sector de Productos Notradicionales," in S. Pathano, ed., *Políticos Agrarias y Empleo en América Latina* (Quito, Ecuador: IEF/ILDIS/CLACSO, 1987), 130.

220. Michael Carter, Bradford Barham, Dina Mesbah, and Denise Stanley, "Agroexports and the Rural Resource Poor in Latin America: Policy Options for Achieving Broadly-Based Growth," draft paper, University of Wisconsin, Land Tenure Center, Madison, Wis., 1993, p. 5.

221. José Mendez, *The Development of the Colombian Cut Flower Industry*, World Bank Working Paper Series 660 (Washington, D.C.: World Bank, Country Economics Department, 1991), 1.

222. Jorge Torres, "Agricultural Modernization and Resource Deterioration in Latin America," draft paper, Interamerican Institute for Cooperation on Agriculture, San José, Costa Rica, 1994, p. 67.

223. James Fox, K. Swanberg, and T. Mehan, "Agribusiness Assessment: The Case of Guatemala," draft paper, U.S. Agency for International Development, Washington, D.C., 1994, p. 30. Another estimate by the Horticultural Guild shows almost three times as many jobs—approximately 112,000 employees—in Guatemala's nontraditional agroexports, but the reliability of these figures is not known.

224. Jürgen Weller, "Las exportaciones agrícolas no tradicionales y sus efectos en el empleo y los ingresos," in Ana Beatriz Mendizábal P. and Jürgen Weller, eds., *Promesa o Espejismo?* (Panama City, Panama: Programa Regional del Empleo para América Latina y el Caribe, 1992), 142.

225. Jürgen Weller, "Las exportaciones agrícolas no tradicionales y sus efectos en el empleo y los ingresos," in Ana Beatriz Mendizábal P. and Jürgen Weller, eds., *Promesa o Espejismo?* (Panama City, Panama: Programa Regional del Empleo para América Latina y el Caribe, 1992), 142.

226. Jürgen Weller, "Las exportaciones agrícolas no tradicionales y sus efectos en el empleo y los ingresos," in Ana Beatriz Mendizábal P. and Jürgen Weller, eds., *Promesa o Espejismo?* (Panama City, Panama: Programa Regional del Empleo para América Latina y el Caribe, 1992), 144.

227. Proyecto para Exportación Agrícola No-Tradicional (PROEXANT) *Informe Anual* (Quito, Ecuador: PROEXANT, 1994); Kenneth Swanberg, "Agribusiness Assessment: Nontraditional Exports in Ecuador," unpublished draft paper, U.S.

Agency for International Development, Center for Development Information and Evaluation, Washington, D.C., 1994.

228. Amalia Alberti, "Impact of Participation in Nontraditional Agricultural Export Production on the Employment, Income, and Quality of Life of Women in Guatemala, Honduras, and Costa Rica," unpublished report, U.S. Agency for International Development, Regional Office for Central America and Panama, Guatemala City, Guatemala, 1991, p. 32.

229. José Mendez, *The Development of the Colombian Cut Flower Industry*, World Bank Working Paper Series 660 (Washington, D.C.: World Bank, Country Economics Department, 1994), 1.

230. Proyecto para Exportación Agrícola No-Tradicional (PROEXANT), "Reporte Anual," unpublished report, PROEXANT, Quito, Ecuador, 1993.

231. Amalia Alberti, "Impact of Participation in Nontraditional Agricultural Export Production on the Employment, Income, and Quality of Life of Women in Guatemala, Honduras, and Costa Rica," unpublished report, U.S. Agency for International Development, Regional Office for Central America and Panama, Guatemala City, Guatemala, 1991, p. 5. Also confirmed in Jürgen Weller, "Las exportaciones agrícolas no tradicionales y sus efectos en el empleo y los ingresos," in Ana Beatriz Mendizábal P. and Jürgen Weller, eds., *Promesa o Espejismo?* (Panama City, Panama: Programa Regional del Empleo para América Latina y el Caribe, 1992), 149.

232. Amalia Alberti, "Impact of Participation in Nontraditional Agricultural Export Production on the Employment, Income, and Quality of Life of Women in Guatemala, Honduras, and Costa Rica," unpublished report, U.S. Agency for International Development, Regional Office for Central America and Panama, Guatemala City, Guatemala, 1991, p. 5.

233. Jürgen Weller, "Las exportaciones agrícolas no tradicionales y sus efectos en el empleo y los ingresos," in Ana Beatriz Mendizábal P. and Jürgen Weller, ed., *Promesa o Espejismo?* (Panama City, Panama: Programa Regional para América Latina y el Caribe, 1992), 149.

234. Lucía Salamea et al., *Rol e Impacto en Mujeres Trabajadoras en Cultivos No-tradicionales para la Exportación en Ecuador* (Quito,

Ecuador: Centro de Planificación y Estudios Sociales, 1993), 24.

235. Rae Blumberg, "Gender and Ecuador's New Export Sectors," draft paper, U.S. Agency for International Development, GENESYS (Gender in Economic and Social Systems) project, Washington, D.C., 1992.

236. Lucía Salamea et al., *Rol e Impacto en Mujeres Trabajadoras en Cultivos No-tradicionales para la Exportación en Ecuador* (Quito, Ecuador: Centro de Planificación y Estudios Sociales, 1993), 24.

237. Rae Blumberg, "Gender and Ecuador's New Export Sectors," draft paper, U.S. Agency for International Development, GENESYS (Gender in Economic and Social Systems) project, Washington, D.C., 1992; Lucía Salamea et al., *Rol e Impacto en Mujeres Trabajadoras en Cultivos No-tradicionales para la Exportación en Ecuador* (Quito, Ecuador: Centro de Planificación y Estudios Sociales, 1993).

238. Wayne Williams, Environmental Officer, U.S. Agency for International Development, Guatemala, personal communication.

239. B. Hess, "Estudios de casos sobre la realidad de la mujer ecuatoriana en sectores críticos del desarrollo," draft paper, Pontífica Universidad Católica del Ecuador, Cuenca, Ecuador, 1990; Rae Blumberg, "Gender and Ecuador's New Export Sectors," draft paper, U.S. Agency for International Development, GENESYS (Gender in Economic and Social Systems) project, Washington, D.C., 1992.

240. Amy Sparks and Bravo-Urea, "Fruit Production in Chile: A Review of Recent Developments," *Journal of International Food and Agribusiness Marketing*, 1992, vol. 4, no. 4:57.

241. Amalia Alberti, "Impact of Participation in Nontraditional Agricultural Export Production on the Employment, Income, and Quality of Life of Women in Guatemala, Honduras, and Costa Rica," unpublished report, U.S. Agency for International Development, Regional Office for Central America and Panama, Guatemala City, Guatemala, 1991, p. 5.

242. Wayne Williams, personal communication, 1993; discussions with smallholders in workshops as part of field studies, 1993.

243. Lucía Salamea et al., *Rol e Impacto en Mujeres Trabajadoras en Cultivos No-tradicionales para la Exportación en Ecuador* (Quito,

Ecuador: Centro de Planificación y Estudios Sociales/Universidad San Francisco de Quito, 1993). See Box 3 for some findings. Other studies include Rae Blumberg, "Gender and Ecuador's New Export Sectors," draft paper, U.S. Agency for International Development, GENESYS Project, Washington,D.C., 1992.

244. Lucía Salamea et al., *Rol e Impacto en Mujeres Trabajadoras En Cultivos No-tradicionales para la Exportación en Ecuador"* (Quito, Ecuador: Centro de Planificación y Estudios Sociales, 1993), 31.

245. Rae Blumberg, "Gender and Ecuador's New Export Sectors," draft paper, U.S. Agency for International Development, GENESYS (Gender in Economic and Social Systems) Project, Washington, D.C., 1992.

246. Jorge Jenrich, *Flower News* (Stuttgart, Germany: Bread for the World, 1992; CUT, "Cuando las Flores Hablan," *Profamilia*, October 1991.

247. Manager of broccoli at a nontraditional agroexport packing company, personal communication, Ecuador, 1993.

248. Krishna Kumar. *Generating Broad-Based Growth Through Agribusiness Promotion.* USAID Program and Operations Assessment Report no. 9. (Washington, D.C.: U.S. Agency for International Development, 1994), p. 34.

249. Proyecto para Exportación Agrícola No-Tradicional, unpublished data, 1993.

250. These kinds of benefits are mentioned in, e.g., Panfilo Tabora, "Central America and South America's Pacific Rim Countries: Experience with Export Diversification," in Shawki Barghouti, L. Garbus, and D. Umali, eds., *Trends in Agricultural Diversification*, World Bank Technical Paper number 180 (Washington, D.C.: World Bank, 1992), 101. Also in Joseph Collins, "Nontraditional Agroexports, Basic Food Crops, and Small Farmers in Central America," unpublished paper, Inter-American Foundation, Arlington, Va., 1992.

251. Safeway, produce marketing data, May 1994.

252. Proyecto para Exportación Agrícola No-Tradicional and Universidad San Francisco de Quito, unpublished data from field survey of nontraditional agroexport farms, Quito, Ecuador, 1993.

253. Production manager, strawberry plantation, personal communication, 1992.

254. Douglas Murray, *Cultivating Crisis: The Human Costs of Pesticides in Central America* (Austin, Tex.: University of Texas, 1994).

255. William F. Waters, "Restructuring of Ecuadorian Agriculture and the Development of Nontraditional Exports: Evidence from the Cut Flower Industry," (Quito: Universidad San Francisco de Quito, 1992). (Paper presented at the 55th Meeting of the Rural Sociological Society, University Park, PA.)

256. CICP, "Environmental Assessment of the Highland Agricultural Development Project," Project Amendment, Phase 2 (College Park, Md.: Consortium for International Crop Protection, 1988).

257. Richard W. Fisher, Roberto Cáceres, Edgardo Cáceres, and Danilo Dardón, "Informe Final: Evaluación del Manejo de Plagas y Plaguicidas en Arveja China del Altiplano de Guatemala," unpublished final report on study by Centro Mesoamericano de Tecnología Apropiada, El Instituto de Ciencia y Tecnología Agrícola, and World Resources Institute, Guatemala City, Guatemala, April 1994.

258. Douglas Murray, *Cultivating Crisis: The Human Costs of Pesticides in Central America* (Austin, Tex.: University of Texas Press, 1994), 67.

259. World Resources Institute analysis of U.S. Food and Drug Administration unpublished detention data, Washington, D.C., 1983–1994.

260. U.S. Food and Drug Administration, primary unpublished data, Washington, D.C., 1983–1994 (analyzed/compiled by World Resources Institute).

261. Douglas Murray and Polly Hoppin, "Recurring Contradictions in Agrarian Development: Pesticide Problems in Caribbean Basin Nontraditional Agriculture," *World Development*, 1992, vol. 20, no. 4:603.

262. Calculation of World Resources Institute, based on analysis of U.S. Food and Drug Administration primary data.

263. World Resources Institute analysis of U.S. Food and Drug Administration unpublished detention data, Washington, D.C., 1983–1994.

264. Douglas Murray and Polly Hoppin, "Recurring Contradictions in Agrarian Development: Pesticide Problems in Caribbean Basin Nontraditional Agriculture," *World Development*, 1992, vol. 20, no. 4:603.

265. Douglas Murray, *Cultivating Crisis: The Human Cost of Pesticides in Central America* (Austin, Tex.: University of Texas Press, 1994), 89.

266. Douglas Murray and Polly Hoppin, "Recurring Contradictions in Agrarian Development: Pesticide Problems in Caribbean Basin Nontraditional Agriculture," *World Development*, 1992, vol. 20, no. 4:603.

267. Douglas Murray and Polly Hoppin, "Recurring Contradictions in Agrarian Development: Pesticide Problems in Caribbean Basin Nontraditional Agriculture," *World Development*, 1992, vol. 20, no. 4:603; Douglas Murray, *Cultivating Crisis: The Human Costs of Pesticides in Central America* (Austin, Tex.: University of Texas Press, 1994).

268. Mauricio Davalos, Exportadores de Flores de Ecuador, Jorge Rodriguez, Proyecto para Exportación Agrícola No-Tradicional, and other decision-makers in export promotion activities, personal communications, Quito, Ecuador, 1993.

269. See, e.g., Lori Ann Thrupp, "Entrapment and Escape from Fruitless Insecticide Use: Lessons from the Banana Sector in Costa Rica," *International Journal of Environmental Studies*, 1990, vol. 36:173–189; Douglas Murray, *Cultivating Crisis: The Human Costs of Pesticides in Central America* (Austin, Tex.: University of Texas Press, 1994); D. Bull, *A Growing Problem: Pesticides and the Third World Poor* (Oxford, U.K.: Oxfam Books, 1982).

270. Francisco Morales, "Controlling Plant Viruses in a Changing Agricultural Environment," unpublished article, Centro Internacional de Agricultura Tropical, Cali, Colombia. Also see Douglas Murray, *Cultivating Crisis: The Human Cost of Pesticides in Central America* (Austin, Tex.: University of Texas Press, 1994).

271. Francisco Morales, "Controlling Plant Viruses in a Changing Agricultural Environment," unpublished article, Centro Internacional de Agricultura Tropical, Cali, Colombia.

272. Douglas Murray, *Cultivating Crisis: The Human Cost of Pesticide Use* (Austin, Tex.: University of Texas Press, 1994), 84.

273. Douglas Murray, *Cultivating Crisis: The Human Cost of Pesticide Use* (Austin, Tex.: University of Texas Press, 1994), 84.
274. Douglas Murray, *Cultivating Crisis: The Human Cost of Pesticide Use* (Austin, Tex.: University of Texas Press, 1994), 79.
275. Douglas Murray, *Cultivating Crisis: The Human Cost of Pesticide Use* (Austin, Tex.: University of Texas Press, 1994), 79.
276. Francisco Morales, Centro Internacional de Agricultura Tropical, personal communication, June 1994.
277. Francisco Morales, "Controlling Plant Viruses in a Changing Agricultural Environment," unpublished article, Centro Internacional de Agricultura Tropical, 1994.
278. Proyecto para Exportación Agrícola No-Tradicional and Universidad San Francisco de Quito, unpublished survey data on pesticide use in nontraditional agroexports, Quito, Ecuador, 1993.
279. Survey by Proyecto para Exportación Agrícola No-Tradicional and Universidad San Francisco de Quito, Quito, Ecuador, 1993.
280. Rae Blumberg, "Gender and Ecuador's New Export Sectors," draft paper, U.S. Agency for International Development, GENESYS Project, Washington, D.C., 1992.
281. World Health Organization (WHO), *Public Health Impact of Pesticides Used in Agriculture* (Geneva: WHO, 1990).
282. David Kaimowitz, personal communication, 1994.
283. Wayne Williams, U.S. Agency for International Development-Guatemala, personal communication, 1994.
284. Maarten Immink, International Food Policy Research Institute, personal communication, September 1994.
285. Mauricio Davalos, personal communication, 1992.
286. Susan Stonich, "The Promotion of Nontraditional Agricultural Exports in Honduras: Issues of Equity, Environment and Natural Resource Management," *Development and Change*, 1991, vol. 22:725–755.
287. Ian Merwin and M. Pritts, "Are Modern Fruit Production Systems Sustainable?", *HortTechnology*, April–June 1993, vol. 3, no. 2:130.
288. Quoted from a U.S. Agency for International Development officer, in Michael Conroy, Douglas Murray, and Peter Rosset,

Fruits of the Crisis. Gambling on Nontraditional Agriculture, unpublished book manuscript. 1994

289. This section is based on Richard W. Fisher, Roberto Cáceres, Edgardo Cáceres, and Danilo Dardón, "Informe Final: Evaluación del Manejo de Plagas y Plaguicidas en Arveja China del Altiplano de Guatemala," unpublished final report on study by Centro Mesoamericano de Tecnología Apropiada, El Instituto de Ciencia y Tecnología Agrícola, and World Resources Institute, Guatemala City, Guatemala, April 1994.

290. Ali Valdivia, Lorena Lastres, and Alfredo Rueda, "Programa MIP-Melon Zamorano en Honduras y Nicaragua, Zamorano (Escuela Panamericana); Louise Shaxson, "Implanting IPM in Central America: Four Case Studies," paper presented at the IPM Working Group workshop, Interamerican Institute for Cooperation on Agriculture, San José, Costa Rica, 1994.

291. Michael Conroy, "Problemas y alternativas económicas a las EANT," in Instituto de Nutrición de Centro América y Panamá (INCAP) and World Resources Institute (WRI), *Sostenabilidad de la Exportación Agrícola No-Tradicional por Pequeños Productores en Guatemala* (Guatemala City, Guatemala: INCAP and WRI, 1994), 36.

292. Michael Conroy, "Problemas y alternativas económicas a las EANT," in Instituto de Nutrición de Centro América y Panamá (INCAP) and World Resources Institute (WRI), *Sostenabilidad de la Exportación Agrícola No-Tradicional por Pequeños Productores en Guatemala* (Guatemala City, Guatemala: INCAP and WRI, 1994), 36; based on U.S. Department of Agriculture data.

293. Kevin Healy, "El Ceibo: Andean Traditional Organization and International Chocolate," *Culture and Development*, 1993, vol. 35.

294. National Cooperative Business Alliance, fact sheet on Cooperative League of the United States of America (CLUSA); Karen Schwartz, personal communication, May 1994.

295. National Cooperative Business Alliance, fact sheet on Cooperative League of the United States of America; Karen Schwartz, personal communication, May 1994.

296. David Griswold and L. von Foerster, Aztec Harvests, personal communication, 1994.

201

297. Paula Palmer, personal communication, 1993 (reporting information on NGOs and grassroots groups in Costa Rica).
298. Paula Palmer, personal communication, 1993 (reporting information on NGOs and grassroots groups in Costa Rica).
299. Michael Carter, B. Barham, and D. Mesbah. "Agroexport Booms and the Rural Resource Poor in Chile, Guatemala, and Paraguay." Unpublished paper. (Madison: University of Wisconsin, 1994) p. 32.

World Resources Institute

The World Resources Institute (WRI) is an independent center for policy research and technical assistance on global environmental and development issues. WRI's mission is to move human society to live in ways that protect Earth's environment and its capacity to provide for the needs and aspirations of current and future generations.

Because people are inspired by ideas, empowered by knowledge, and moved to change by greater understanding, the Institute provides—and helps other institutions provide—objective information and practical proposals for policy and institutional change that will foster environmentally sound, socially equitable development. WRI's particular concerns are with globally significant environmental problems and their interaction with economic development and social equity at all levels.

The Institute's current areas of work include economics, forests, biodiversity, climate change, energy, sustainable agriculture, resource and environmental information, trade, technology, national strategies for environmental and resource management, and human health.

In all of its policy research and work with institutions, WRI tries to build bridges between ideas and action, meshing the insights of scientific research, economic and institutional analyses, and practical experience with the need for open and participatory decision-making.